NINJA CREAMI
DELUXE PROTEIN
COOKBOOK

Your Ultimate Guide to Healthy Ice Creams, Milkshakes, and More Frozen Treats for Summer

ANN J. BRYNER

COPYRIGHT © 2024 ANN J. BRYNER

Welcome to your Ninja Creami Deluxe Protein Adventure. This cookbook is your trusty sidekick, whether you are a gym buff, a busy parent, or someone who simply loves guilt-free treats. Get ready to whip up protein-packed frozen goodness that is both delicious and good for you.

Before We Dig In:

Take a minute to get to know your Ninja Creami Deluxe. Think of it like learning the controls of a spaceship before blasting off into the cosmos! Once you have the basics down, you will be a frozen treat wizard in no time. In addition, if you are new to this whole thing, do not worry; we have got you covered with a crash course in the first chapter.

Find Your Flavor:

Flip through this cookbook and let your cravings guide you. When you see a recipe that makes you drool; Bookmark it! Feel free to mix and match flavors, swap out ingredients, and get creative. I encourage you to play and make these recipes your own.

Numbers Matter (But Taste Matters More):

At the start of each recipe, I have listed the good stuff: calories, protein, fat, and carbs. This helps you choose treats that fit your goals, whether that is fueling a workout or just satisfying a sweet tooth. However, remember, the most important thing is that it tastes amazing!

Level Up Your Ninja Skills:

Start with the basic recipes to get the hang of things. Once you are a pro, it is time to unleash your inner chef! Combine flavors, adjust the sweetness, and even add surprise ingredients.

Who Said Ice Cream Was Just for Dessert?

Surprise! The Ninja Creami is not just for sweet treats. I will show you how to use it for healthy frozen yogurt bowls, protein-packed Milkshakes, and even some savory surprises.

This cookbook is more than just recipes, it is your ticket to a healthier, happier you. So, get your Ninja Creami fired up, stock up on your favorite protein powder, and let us make some magic together!

TABLE OF CONTENTS

INTRODUCTION TO NINJA CREAMI DELUXE PROTEIN COOKBOOK 11

GETTING STARTED WITH NINJA CREAMI DELUXE 13

Key Features Include 13

What Sets the Ninja Creami Deluxe Apart? 13

Functions of the Ninja Creami Deluxe 13

Cleaning & Maintenance 14

Mix-In Tips 14

Benefits of Protein-Packed Recipes 14

Tips for Using the Ninja Creami Deluxe 14

Essential Ingredients for High-Protein Treats 14

Natural Protein Powerhouses 15

Sweetness & Flavor 15

The Key to Creaminess 15

Getting the Most Out of Your Machine 16

Troubleshooting 16

SCOOPABLE SUMMER TREATS: PROTEIN POWER-UP ICE CREAMS 17

Peachy Protein Dream Ice Cream 17

Pineapple Coconut Protein Swirl Ice Cream 18

Watermelon Mint Refresher Ice Cream 19

Peanut Butter Cup Obsession Ice Cream 20

Minty Chocolate Chip Protein Ice Cream 21

Cookies & Cream Protein Dream Ice Cream 22

Chocolate Brownie Batter Protein Shake Ice Cream 23

Strawberry Cheesecake Protein Shake Ice Cream...24

Vanilla Bean Protein Ice Cream...25

Coffee Caramel Protein Ice Cream..26

SCOOPABLE GELATO SUMMER SURPRISE   27

Berry Balsamic Protein Swirl...27

Strawberry Kiwi Protein Swirl...28

Stracciatella Protein...29

Tropical Passion Fruit...29

Vanilla Chai Protein Shake..30

Honey Lavender Protein Gelato...31

Protein Powerhouse Pistachio..32

Keto Coffee Gelato...33

Hazelnut Chocolate Swirl Protein Gelato..34

Chunky Monkey Protein Gelato...35

REFRESHING SUMMER SORBET TREATS   37

Tropical Protein Punch Sorbet...37

Chocolate Peanut Butter Protein Sorbet..38

Berry Vanilla Protein Swirl Sorbet...39

Creamy Coconut Sorbet..40

Strawberry Summer Sorbet..41

Mango Lassi Sorbet..42

Protein Blast Berry Mix Sorbet..43

Tropical Protein Paradise Sorbet..43

Tart Cherry Protein Power Sorbet...44

Raspberry-Lime Protein Fizz Sorbet...46

SCOOPABLE SUMMER LITE ICE CREAM 47

Citrus Sunshine protein Lite Ice 47

Salted Caramel Mocha Protein Lite Ice Protein 48

Matcha Coconut Cream Protein Lite Ice 49

Tropical Piña Colada Protein Lite Ice 50

Low Carb Mint Madness Protein Lite Ice 51

Low-Calorie Brownie Chunk Protein Lite Ice 52

Vegan Vanilla Protein Base 53

Protein Coffee Lite Ice Cream 54

SUMMER CREAMY PROTEIN FROZEN YOGHURT 55

Greek Yogurt Protein Base 55

Tropical Protein Yogurt Delight 56

Peach Melba Swirl 57

High-Protein Parfait 58

Berry Banana Protein Yogurt Delight 59

Probiotic Protein Boost 60

Green Protein Fro-Yo 61

Berry Banana Protein Yogurt Delight 63

SUMMER ITALIAN ICE TREATS 65

Dragon Fruit Protein Delight 65

Strawberry Lemonade Protein Fusion 66

Pineapple Jalapeno Protein Surprise 67

Spiced Apple Protein Cider 68

Root Beer Protein Float 69

Horchata Protein Spice 70

Coconut Cream Protein Pie 71

Mixed Berry Protein Refresher 72

Coconut Cardamom Protein Bliss 73

Chocolate Banana Protein 74

DRINKABLE SUMMER TREATS: MILKSHAKE WITH MUSCLE 75

Fruity Fiesta Protein Shake 75

Minty Chocolate Chip Protein Shake 75

Coffee Lover's Protein Pick-Me-Up 76

Oatmeal Cookie Protein Shake 77

Double Chocolate Malt 78

Cookies & Cream Protein Overload 79

Almond Joy Protein Shake 80

Raspberry Cheesecake Protein Shake 81

Mango Pineapple Protein Shake 82

Build-Your-Own Protein Shake 83

DRINKABLE SUMMER CREAMICCINO TREATS 84

Blueberry Muffin Protein 84

Citrus Buzz Protein 85

Creamiccino 85

Raspberry Cocoa Protein Creamiccino 86

Caramel Apple Protein Creamiccino 87

Pumpkin Spice Protein Creamiccino 88

Maple Cinnamon Latte Protein Creamiccino 89

SUMMER FROZEN DRINK TREATS 90

Sunrise Protein Smoothie 90

Frozen Protein Mudslide 91

Watermelon Protein Frosé 92

Spiced Pear & Ginger Protein Shake 93

Green Machine Protein Shake 94

Banana Bread Protein Shake 95

Coffee Toffee Crunch Protein Shake 96

Gingerbread Protein Shake 97

Strawberry Shortcake Protein Shake 98

Black Forest Protein Shake 99

REFRESHING SLUSHY SUMMER TREATS   100

Pink Lemonade Protein Slushy 100

Pineapple Mango Protein Slushy 101

Sweet Cream Protein Slushy 102

Pineapple Green Tea Protein Slushy 103

Peachy Protein Zing 104

Green Machine Protein Slush 105

Raspberry Rosé Sparkler 106

Bellini Bliss Slushy 107

Dragon Fruit Lime Zing Slush 108

VEGAN PROTEIN POWER FOR NINJA CREAMI CREATIONS   109

The Vegan Protein Pantry 109

Creamy Vegan Secrets 109

Keto Creami Craze 109

Sugar-Free Symphony 109

Dairy-Free Delights 109

Frozen Treats, Keto Style 110

Chocolate Avocado Fudge Pops 110

Strawberry Cheesecake Ice Cream 111

Vanilla Bean Ice Cream 111

Lemon Coconut Cream Pops 112

Ninja Creami Hacks 113

ACKNOWLEDGEMENT 114

BONUS SECTION: PROTEIN PACKED 14-DAY MEALPLAN 115

NINJA CREAMI RECIPE TRACKER 117

APPENDIX 1: RECIPE INDEX 123

APPENDIX 2: CONVERSION CHART 125

INTRODUCTION TO NINJA CREAMI DELUXE PROTEIN COOKBOOK

Can you remember those scorching summer days as a kid, begging for ice cream trucks to meander down your street? The sweet, creamy symphony of flavors burst onto your tongue with every lick; pure, unadulterated bliss. However, as we grow older, those carefree indulgences often come with a side of guilt. Sugar crashes, unwanted pounds, and the nagging feeling that we are sabotaging all our health efforts.

That is exactly how I felt. I craved delicious frozen treats, but the store-bought options left me unsatisfied, in terms of both taste and nutrition. Then, a friend introduced me to the magical world of the Ninja Creami Deluxe. It was not just an ice cream maker; it was a portal back to my childhood joy but with an adult twist, the power to create protein-packed frozen delights!

Skeptical at first, I whipped up a simple vanilla protein ice cream. The first spoonful was a revelation. It was creamy, smooth, and packed with that classic vanilla bean flavor, but without the guilt. The protein /content kept me satiated, and the sugar level was perfectly balanced – no more afternoon crashes! My journey into the world of Ninja Creami protein treats had begun.

However, the Ninja Creami Deluxe is not just about ice cream. Ninja creami is a versatile machine that unlocks a whole spectrum of frozen treats like milkshakes, gelatos, sorbets and slushies. The possibilities were endless. I experimented with fruity concoctions, decadent chocolate swirls, and refreshing protein-infused smoothies. My freezer transformed into a wonderland of self-made treats, each one a delicious adventure.

The impact on my health was undeniable. I started craving natural ingredients, and by controlling the sugar content, I felt a surge in energy. I could luxuriate in a sweet treat without compromising my fitness goals. It was a revelation: delicious frozen treats could be part of a healthy lifestyle!

However, navigating the vast world of Ninja Creami recipes can be daunting. Many require obscure ingredients or intricate techniques. This cookbook was born out of that desire for simplicity. I want everyone to experience the joy and health benefits of Ninja Creami protein treats, regardless of the experience we have.

"The Ninja Creami Deluxe Protein Cookbook" offers a unique approach. I focused on creating flavorful and accessible recipes using readily available ingredients. With detailed instructions and clear explanations, even beginners can become Ninja Creami masters.

This book goes beyond just recipes. I will guide you through the key principles behind protein-powered frozen treats, tailoring them to the health-conscious lifestyle so prevalent today. You will find tips on choosing the right protein powder, balancing sweetness naturally, and incorporating healthy fats and fruits.

I believe everyone deserves a sweet escape, a chance to revel without sacrificing health. With "The Ninja Creami Deluxe Protein Cookbook" as your guide, you can unlock a world of delicious possibilities. So, grab your Ninja Creami, turn the page, and let us venture on a delectable journey together!

The Ninja Creami Deluxe is a revolutionary kitchen appliance that transforms frozen ingredients into ice cream, sorbets, milkshakes, smoothies, and more all in a matter of minutes! It sets itself apart from traditional ice cream makers with its ease of use and versatility.

Key Features Include

- **Pre-Freezing**: Instead of a built-in freezing bowl, the Creami Deluxe uses pre-frozen pints for its base. Simply mix your ingredients, freeze for 24 hours, and churn!

- **Powerful Blade**: The Creami's specially designed blade shaves and churns your frozen pint, creating a creamy, scoopable consistency.

- **Multiple Functions**: Choose from dedicated settings for Ice Cream, Sorbet, Milkshakes, and more, making it simple to create your favorite treats.

What Sets the Ninja Creami Deluxe Apart?

- **Customization**: Control the ingredients for healthier homemade treats, and cater to dietary restrictions or special preferences.

- **Speed and Convenience**: Get fresh, custom ice cream in minutes, compared to hours with many traditional machines.

- **Versatility**: Go beyond basic ice cream with a wide array of frozen treats at your fingertips.

Functions of the Ninja Creami Deluxe

- **Ice Cream**: Create classic, creamy ice creams in endless flavors.

- **Lite Ice Cream**: Lower-sugar, lower-calorie ice cream options.

- **Sorbet**: Refreshing fruit-based frozen desserts.

- **Gelato**: Dense, flavorful Italian-style ice cream.

- **Milkshake**: Thick and indulgent shakes.

- **Mix-In**: Conveniently add candies, cookies, and other goodies during the final minute of churning.

- **Slushy**: Make your favorite slushy flavors right at home.

- **Frozen Drink**: Perfect for frozen cocktails and other adult beverages.

- **Frozen Yogurt**: Creamy and tangy frozen yogurt variations

- **Italian Ice**: Smooth, flavorful water-based Italian ice treat.

- **Creamiccino**: Cafe-style blended coffee drinks.

Cleaning & Maintenance

- **Easy Cleanup**: The Creami Deluxe components (pint, lid, and blade) are dishwasher-safe for quick and effortless cleaning.
- **Blade Maintenance**: Occasional rinsing and drying the blade thoroughly will help extend its lifespan.

Mix-In Tips

- **Size Matters**: Larger mix-ins like cookie chunks work best if broken into smaller pieces.
- **Timing is Key**: Use the Mix-In function in the last minute of processing for optimal distribution.
- **Get Creative**: Mix-ins do not have to be sweet! Try savory additions like pretzel bits or crumbled potato chips.

Benefits of Protein-Packed Recipes

- **Muscle Building**: Protein supports muscle growth and repair.
- **Satiety**: Feel fuller for longer, helping manage cravings.
- **Overall Health**: Protein is an essential nutrient for many bodily functions.

Tips for Using the Ninja Creami Deluxe

- **Read the manual** and familiarize yourself with the various settings and troubleshooting tips.
- **Freeze Properly**: Ensure your base is completely solid before processing.
- **Do not overfill**: Adhere to the fill line on the pints for the best results.
- **Re-Spin if needed** for a firmer consistency; utilize the re-spin function.
- Experiment and Have Fun! The Creami is all about unleashing your creativity in the kitchen

Essential Ingredients for High-Protein Treats

- **Whey Protein**: the body absorbs the Classic Choice Derived from milk, whey quickly, making it ideal post-workout. It often comes in a wide variety of flavors and mixes easily into liquids.
- **Casein Protein**: The Slow-Burner Also from milk, casein digests more slowly, providing a sustained release of protein. It is a good choice before bed or if skipping meals. You may notice a thicker texture.
- **Vegan Options**: Plant Power! Pea, rice, hemp, and soy protein powders offer

complete amino acid profiles, catering to plant-based preferences. Pay attention to flavor, as these can be earthier and work best mixed with strong flavors.

Choosing the Right Protein Powder

- **Fitness Goals**: For active lifestyles, whey is versatile. Casein is good for extended recovery. Vegan options work wonders if following that lifestyle.
- **Taste Test**: Samples are your friend! Some flavors are sweeter, others more neutral. Find a protein powder you genuinely enjoy the taste.
- **Dietary Needs**: Check for allergens (lactose, soy, etc.). Many brands offer options for specific sensitivities.

Natural Protein Powerhouses

- **Greek Yogurt**: Creamy & Tangy Adds a protein punch, creates a thick base, and offers a bit of tartness that balances sweeter flavors.
- **Kefir**: Probiotic Boost! Similar to drinkable yogurt, kefir provides protein, good bacteria, and a unique tang.
- **Nuts and Seeds**: Flavor and Crunch: Cashews, almonds, sunflower seeds...the list is endless! While whole nuts work as mix-ins, nut/seed butters lend

creaminess and extra protein to the base itself.

- **Silken Tofu**: The Secret Weapon: Surprisingly versatile, silken tofu blends smoothly, adding protein and thickness. It is particularly well suited for vegan and dairy-sensitive recipes.

Sweetness & Flavor

- **Sugar Substitutes**: Less Sweetness, More Control: Stevia, erythritol, or monk fruit extract offer sweetness without the sugar spike.
- **Nature is Candy**: Maple syrup, Honey, & Dates these bring natural sweetness and unique flavor profiles.
- **Fruit Power**: Double Duty Frozen berries, bananas, mangoes not only add sweetness and flavor, but also pack in fiber and essential nutrients.

The Key to Creaminess

- **Avocados**: Rich and Creamy their healthy fats transform your treats into decadent delights. They are particularly delicious in chocolate or tropical flavors.
- **Nut Butters**: Flavor and Fat Peanut butter, almond butter, and more are staples! Just a small spoonful goes a long way in enriching your frozen dessert.

Getting the Most Out of Your Machine

Master the Basics:

- **Freezing**: Stress the 24-hour minimum freeze time and that SOLID frozen is non-negotiable.

- **Cycles**: Clearly describe the initial cycle time for different settings, what the Creami sounds like when done, and how to tell if your dessert needs more processing.

- **Understanding Texture**: Talk about soft-serve versus scoopable. That different treats have ideal consistencies (sorbet is less firm than ice cream naturally).

Re-Spin Secrets:

- **Why Re-spin**: It is not mandatory, but re-spinning gives firmer and more consistent ice cream textures.

- **When to Do It**: Say how ONCE the initial cycle is done, you can re-spin immediately, or pop it back in the freezer to firm up as needed. Multiple re-spins may be the answer for some recipes.

Mix-ins Magic:

- **Timing**: The MIX-IN button has its own cycle, designed with the last minute in mind to prevent pulverizing your mix-ins.

- **Size and Texture**: Explain larger brownie chunks are broken, and that very soft mix-ins will not incorporate the same way. Give examples!

- **Sweet and Savory**: Do not limit mix-ins to cookies and candy. Talk about savory ideas like pretzels, crumbled bacon, etc., for surprising twists.

Troubleshooting

- **Too icy**: causes like not freezing long enough, overly wet base, or adding alcohol (lowers freezing point).

- **Too Soft**: Sometimes the base is not solid enough or ingredients are too warm. Stress freezing well and potentially chilling your ingredients before mixing.

- **Grainy**: Could be because of low-quality protein powder or ice crystals from

- **Improper freezing**. Emphasize choosing smoother protein powders and proper freezing methods.

"Savor the flavors of success with each creamy."

Peachy Protein Dream Ice Cream

Enjoy a delightful summer treat with this Peachy Protein Dream ice cream! This delicious dessert combines peaches, Greek yogurt, and protein powder for a healthier twist on a creamy, refreshing favorite.

INGREDIENTS

- 1 cup frozen peaches
- 1/2 cup plain Greek yogurt
- 1 scoop vanilla protein powder
- 1 tablespoon maple syrup
- Toasted sliced almonds (optional, for mix-ins)

Prep Time: 5 minutes Skill Level: Easy

Freezing Time: 24 hours Servings: 2

INSTRUCTIONS

1. In a blender, combine frozen peaches, Greek yogurt, protein powder, and maple syrup. Blend until smooth.
2. Transfer the mixture to a Ninja Creami pint container. Freeze for at least 24 hours.
3. Place the frozen pint in the Ninja Creami Deluxe and select the "Ice Cream" program. Process until it reaches a soft-serve consistency.
4. **Mix-In (Optional)**: Make a small hole in the center of the ice cream to add toasted sliced almonds. Use the "Mix-in" program to incorporate.
5. **Re-spin (Optional)**: For a firmer texture, especially after adding mix-ins, select the "Ice Cream" program again.

HEALTH BENEFITS

- **Vitamins**: High in vitamins A and C, crucial for immune support and skin health.
- **Protein**: Rich in protein, which supports muscle repair and growth.

HEALTHY TIPS

- **Yogurt**: Using plain Greek yogurt increases protein while reducing sugar intake.

Nutritional Information (Per Serving): Calories: 200 Fat: 6g Carbohydrates: 22g Protein: 16g

Pineapple Coconut Protein Swirl Ice Cream

Savor the tropical flavors with this Pineapple Coconut Protein Swirl ice cream. Combining creamy coconut milk, tangy pineapple, and protein powder, this ice cream is a delightful, health-conscious treat.

INGREDIENTS

- 1 cup frozen pineapple chunks
- 1/2 cup coconut milk
- 1 scoop coconut-flavored protein powder
- 1 tablespoon agave syrup
- Shredded coconut (optional, for mix-ins)

Prep Time: 5 minutes Skill Level: Easy

Freezing Time: 24 hours Servings: 2

INSTRUCTIONS

1. In a blender, mix frozen pineapple chunks, coconut milk, protein powder, and agave syrup until the mixture is smooth.
2. Transfer the mixture into a Ninja Creami pint container. Freeze for at least 24 hours.
3. Insert the frozen pint into the Ninja Creami Deluxe and select the "Ice Cream" setting. Let the machine run until the texture becomes soft-serve.
4. Mix-In (Optional): Create a small well in the center of the soft ice cream to add shredded coconut. Select the "Mix-in" program to blend evenly.
5. Re-spin (Optional): For a firmer texture, especially after adding mix-ins, run the "Ice Cream" program once more.

HEALTH BENEFITS

- **Hydration and Electrolytes**: Coconut milk is a good source of hydration and provides essential electrolytes.
- **Vitamins**: Pineapple is rich in vitamin C and manganese, supporting immune function and bone health.

HEALTHY TIPS

- **Coconut Milk**: Using coconut milk adds a creamy texture and can be a lactose-free alternative to traditional dairy.
- **Sweetener**: Agave syrup provides a lower glycemic index alternative to regular sweeteners, which can be better for maintaining blood sugar levels.

Nutritional Information (Per Serving): Calories: 230 Fat: 10g Carbohydrates: 26g Protein: 12g

Watermelon Mint Refresher Ice Cream

Refresh yourself on a hot day with this Watermelon Mint Refresher ice cream. This unique blend of juicy watermelon, fresh mint, and protein powder is not only invigorating but also a healthy treat.

INGREDIENTS

- 1 cup frozen watermelon chunks
- 1/2 cup Greek yogurt
- 1 scoop vanilla protein powder
- 1 tablespoon honey
- Toasted sliced almonds(for mix-ins)

Prep Time: 5 minutes Skill Level: Easy

Freezing Time: 24 hours Servings: 2

INSTRUCTIONS

1. Combine the frozen watermelon, Greek yogurt, protein powder, and honey in a blender. Add a few mint leaves for a refreshing flavor. Blend until smooth.
2. Pour the mixture into a Ninja Creami pint container and freeze for at least 24 hours.
3. Insert the frozen pint into your Ninja Creami Deluxe and select the "Ice Cream" setting. Process until it achieves a soft-serve consistency.
4. Mix-In (Optional): After the initial creamify cycle; add toasted sliced almonds to the center of the ice cream. Use the "Mix-in" program to incorporate evenly.
5. Re-spin (Optional): If you desire a firmer texture, especially after adding mix-ins, run the "Ice Cream" program again.

HEALTH BENEFITS

- Hydration: Watermelon is excellent for hydration, making it perfect for summer.
- Digestive Aid: Mint not only enhances flavor but also aids in digestion.

HEALTHY TIPS

- Yogurt: Opt for low-fat Greek yogurt to maintain a creamy texture while keeping calories low.
- Sweetener: Honey adds natural sweetness and can be adjusted based on your preference for sweetness.

Nutritional Information (Per Serving): Calories: 180 | Fat: 2g | Carbohydrates: 24g | Protein: 15g

Equipment: Blender, Ninja Creami Deluxe, Bowl, Spatula

Peanut Butter Cup Obsession Ice Cream

Luxuriate in the rich and creamy flavor of Peanut Butter Cup Obsession ice cream. This dessert combines the goodness of peanut butter and chocolate protein powder for a decadent, protein-packed treat.

INGREDIENTS:

- 1 cup frozen banana slices
- 1/2 cup plain Greek yogurt
- 1 scoop chocolate protein powder
- 2 tablespoons peanut butter
- Mini chocolate chips or chopped peanuts (optional, for mix-ins)

Prep Time: 5 minutes Skill Level: Easy

Freezing Time: 24 hours Servings: 2

INSTRUCTIONS

1. Combine frozen banana slices, Greek yogurt, chocolate protein powder, and peanut butter in a blender. Blend the ingredients together until they form a smooth, creamy consistency.
2. Transfer the mixture into a Ninja Creami pint container. Make sure not to overfill. Freeze for at least 24 hours.
3. Insert the frozen pint into the Ninja Creami Deluxe and select the "Ice Cream" program. Process until it reaches a soft-serve consistency.
4. Mix-In (Optional): Create a small hole in the center of the soft ice cream to add mini chocolate chips or chopped peanuts. Select the "Mix-in" program to blend evenly.
5. Re-spin (Optional): For a firmer texture, especially after adding mix-ins, run the "Ice Cream" program again.

HEALTH BENEFITS

- **Protein and Healthy Fats**: Peanut butter provides healthy fats and protein, essential for muscle repair and satiety.
- **Potassium**: Bananas are rich in potassium, which supports heart health and muscle function.

HEALTHY TIPS

- **Peanut Butter**: Use natural peanut butter with no added sugars or oils for a healthier option.
- **Sweetener**: The natural sweetness from bananas reduces the need for additional sweeteners.

Nutritional Information (Per Serving):
Calories: 300 | Fat: 14g | Carbohydrates: 30g | Protein: 18g

Minty Chocolate Chip Protein Ice Cream

Experience the refreshing taste of mint combined with rich chocolate chips in this Minty

INGREDIENTS

- 1 cup frozen spinach (for natural green color and nutrients)
- 1/2 cup Greek yogurt
- 1 scoop vanilla protein powder
- 2 tablespoons honey
- 1 teaspoon peppermint extract
- 1/4 cup mini chocolate chips (dark chocolate, for mix-ins)

Prep Time: 5 minutes Skill Level: Easy

Freezing Time: 24 hours Servings: 2

INSTRUCTIONS

1. In a blender, combine the frozen spinach, Greek yogurt, vanilla protein powder, honey, and peppermint extract. Blend until the mixture is smooth and evenly green.
2. Pour the smooth mixture into a Ninja Creami pint container. Be careful not to overfill. Freeze for at least 24 hours.
3. Place the frozen pint into the Ninja Creami Deluxe. Select the "Ice Cream" setting. Let the machine run until it achieves a soft-serve consistency.
4. Mix-In (Optional): Add the mini chocolate chips to the center of the soft ice cream. Choose the "Mix-in" function to ensure the chips are evenly distributed.
5. Re-spin (Optional): If a firmer consistency is desired, especially after adding the chocolate chips, run the "Ice Cream" program again.

HEALTH BENEFITS

- **Antioxidants:** Dark chocolate is a good source of antioxidants, which help protect the body from oxidative stress.
- **Vitamins and Minerals**: Spinach adds vitamins A, C, K, iron, and magnesium, promoting overall health.

HEALTHY TIPS:

- Spinach: Using spinach adds nutrients without altering the flavor significantly due to its mild taste when frozen.
- Peppermint Extract: A little goes a long way, so adjust according to your taste preference for that fresh minty flavor.

Nutritional Information (Per Serving): Calories: 280 | Fat: 10g | Carbohydrates: 32g | Protein: 20g

Cookies & Cream Protein Dream Ice Cream

Get absorbed into the classic delight of cookies and cream with a protein-packed twist. This Cookies & Cream Protein Dream ice cream is both indulgent and nourishing, making it a fantastic treat for any time of the day.

INGREDIENTS

- 1 cup low-fat milk
- 1/2 cup Greek yogurt
- 1 scoop cookies & cream protein powder
- 2 tablespoons crushed low-fat chocolate cookies
- 1 tablespoon agave syrup

Prep Time: 5 minutes Skill Level: Easy

Freezing Time: 24 hours Servings: 2

Skill Level: Easy

INSTRUCTIONS

1. In a blender, mix low-fat milk, Greek yogurt, cookies & cream protein powder, and agave syrup until smooth.
2. Transfer the blended mixture into a Ninja Creami pint container. Avoid overfilling. Freeze for at least 24 hours.
3. Insert the frozen pint into the Ninja Creami Deluxe and select the "Ice Cream" program. Process until it reaches a soft-serve consistency.
4. Mix-In (Optional): After creamifying, add crushed chocolate cookies into the center of the soft ice cream. Use the "Mix-in" program to incorporate evenly.
5. Re-spin (Optional): For a firmer texture, particularly after adding the cookies, select the "Ice Cream" program again.

HEALTH BENEFITS

- Protein: High protein content helps in muscle repair and satiety.
- Calcium: Milk and Greek yogurt provide calcium, essential for bone health.

HEALTHY TIPS:

- Low-Fat Dairy: Using low-fat milk and yogurt reduces overall calorie content while maintaining creaminess.
- Cookies: Opt for low-fat chocolate cookies to keep the dessert lighter.

Nutritional Information (Per Serving): Calories: 220 | Fat: 6g | Carbohydrates: 25g | Protein: 15g

Chocolate Brownie Batter Protein Shake Ice Cream

Delight in the decadent taste of Chocolate Brownie Batter Protein Shake ice cream, perfect for those who crave a rich chocolate experience while getting a good dose of protein.

INGREDIENTS

- 1 cup frozen banana slices
- 1/2 cup Greek yogurt
- 1 scoop chocolate protein powder
- 2 tablespoons unsweetened cocoa powder
- Mini chocolate chips (optional, for mix-ins)

Prep Time: 5 minutes Skill Level: Easy

Freezing Time: 24 hours Servings: 2

Skill Level: Easy

INSTRUCTIONS

1. In a blender, combine banana slices, Greek yogurt, chocolate protein powder, and cocoa powder. Blend until smooth.
2. Transfer the blended mixture into a Ninja Creami pint container. Freeze for at least 24 hours.
3. Use the "Ice Cream" setting on the Ninja Creami Deluxe to achieve a soft-serve consistency.
4. Mix-In (Optional): Add mini chocolate chips and select the "Mix-in" program to distribute evenly.
5. Re-spin (Optional): For a firmer texture, especially after adding mix-ins, run the "Ice Cream" program again.

HEALTH BENEFITS

- Antioxidants: Cocoa powder is rich in antioxidants that help combat free radicals.
- Muscle Recovery: High protein content aids in muscle recovery post-exercise.

HEALTHY TIPS

- Cocoa Quality: Use high-quality, unsweetened cocoa powder to maximize health benefits and control sugar intake.
- Natural Sweeteners: Opt for natural sweeteners like banana or add a touch of honey or maple syrup if additional sweetness is desired.

Nutritional Information (Per Serving):
Calories: 310 | Fat: 6g | Carbohydrates: 42g |

Strawberry Cheesecake Protein Shake Ice Cream

Enjoy the creamy and delightful taste of Strawberry Cheesecake Protein Shake ice cream, combining the classic cheesecake flavor with a nutritional twist.

INGREDIENTS

- 1 cup frozen strawberries
- 1/2 cup Greek yogurt
- 1 scoop vanilla protein powder
- 2 tablespoons cream cheese
- Graham cracker crumbs (optional, for mix-ins)

Prep Time: 5 minutes Skill Level: Easy

Freezing Time: 24 hours Servings: 2

INSTRUCTIONS:

1. Mix frozen strawberries, Greek yogurt, vanilla protein powder, and cream cheese in a blender until creamy.
2. Transfer the blended mixture to a Ninja Creami pint container and freeze for at least 24 hours.
3. Select the "Ice Cream" program on the Ninja Creami Deluxe and process to a soft-serve texture.
4. Mix-In (Optional): Add graham cracker crumbs using the "Mix-in" function for an authentic cheesecake experience.
5. Re-spin (Optional): Run the "Ice Cream" program again for a firmer texture after adding mix-ins.

HEALTH BENEFITS:

- Vitamin C: Strawberries are a great source of vitamin C, which supports immune health.
- Bone Health: Greek yogurt provides calcium for bone strength.

HEALTHY TIPS:

- Reduced Fat Cream Cheese: Use reduced-fat or Neufchatel cheese to lower overall fat content without sacrificing flavor.
- Whole Grain Crumbs: Opt for whole grain graham crackers for a healthier mix-in option.

Nutritional Information (Per Serving): Calories: 290 | Fat: 8g | Carbohydrates: 36g | Protein: 20g

Vanilla Bean Protein Ice Cream

Experience the smooth and classic flavor of Vanilla Bean Protein Ice Cream, an excellent choice for a simple yet satisfying protein-rich dessert.

INGREDIENTS

- 1 cup frozen banana slices

- 1/2 cup Greek yogurt

- 1 scoop vanilla protein powder

- 1 teaspoon vanilla bean paste

Prep Time: 5 minutes Skill Level: Easy

Freezing Time: 24 hours Servings: 2

Skill Level: Easy

INSTRUCTIONS:

1. Combine banana slices, Greek yogurt, vanilla protein powder, and vanilla bean paste in a blender. Blend until smooth.

2. Transfer the blended mixture to a Ninja Creami pint container. Freeze for at least 24 hours.

3. Use the "Ice Cream" setting on your Ninja Creami Deluxe to process the mixture until it achieves a soft-serve consistency.

4. Re-spin (Optional): Run the "Ice Cream" program again for a firmer texture after adding mix-ins.

HEALTH BENEFITS:

- Mood Improvement: Vanilla is known for its calming properties and can help reduce stress.

- Protein and Digestive Health: High protein from the Greek yogurt aids in muscle repair, while probiotics support gut health.

HEALTHY TIPS:

- Vanilla Bean Paste: Opt for real vanilla bean paste for a richer flavor and added nutritional benefits over artificial vanilla.

- Probiotic-Rich Yogurt: Choose yogurt with live cultures for the best health benefits.

Nutritional Information (Per Serving):
Calories: 210 | Fat: 2g | Carbohydrates: 30g | Protein

Coffee Caramel Protein Ice Cream

Wake up and conquer your day with a creamy Coffee Caramel Protein Ice Cream! Imagine the boldness of your favorite coffee combined with the decadent sweetness of caramel, all packed into a protein-rich scoop. This is not just a treat for your taste buds; it is a power-up for your morning routine.

Prep Time: 5 minutes

Freezing Time: 24 hours Servings:

Servings: 2

Skill Level: Easy

INGREDIENTS

- 2 scoops of your go-to coffee-flavored protein powder
- 1 cup of unsweetened almond milk (or your preferred milk alternative)
- 1 tablespoon of sugar-free caramel syrup (the good stuff!)
- 1 teaspoon of instant coffee granules
- A touch of sweetener (optional, to your liking)

- Mix-ins: Chopped nuts, dark chocolate chips, or a sprinkle of cinnamon

HEALTH BENEFITS

- **Coffee-Flavored Protein Powder:** A great source of protein for building and maintaining muscle mass. The caffeine in coffee can also provide a boost of energy and improve focus.

INSTRUCTIONS:

1. Combine all the ingredients into your blender and give it a whirl until everything is smooth and dreamy.
2. Pop that mixture into your Ninja Creami pint container and let it chill out in the freezer for a good 24 hours.
3. Once it has frozen solid, let the Ninja Creami work its magic! Select the "Ice Cream" setting and press start.
4. If you like it extra velvety smooth, give it a "Re-spin" after the first cycle.

HEALTHY TIPS

- **Use unsweetened almond milk or a fortified milk alternative:** This will reduce the sugar content and provide additional vitamins and minerals.

"Transform your kitchen into a ninja training ground."

Berry Balsamic Protein Swirl

Delight in the sophisticated blend of tangy and sweet with this Berry Balsamic Protein Swirl Gelato. This dessert marries the rich flavor of balsamic glaze with the natural sweetness of mixed berries and the nutritional benefits of protein powder for a uniquely delightful treat.

INGREDIENTS

- 1 cup frozen mixed berries (strawberries, raspberries, blueberries)
- 1/2 cup milk (any kind)
- 1 scoop vanilla protein powder
- 2 tablespoons balsamic glaze
- Almonds or walnuts (for mix-ins)

Prep Time: 5 minutes Skill Level: Easy

Freezing Time: 24 hours Servings: 2

INSTRUCTIONS

1. Combine the frozen mixed berries, milk, protein powder, and balsamic glaze in a blender. Blend until smooth.
2. Transfer the blended mixture to a Ninja Creami pint container, ensuring not to overfill. Freeze for at least 24 hours.
3. Gelato Function: Insert the frozen pint into your Ninja Creami Deluxe and select the "Gelato" function. Process until the mixture is creamy.
4. Mix-In (Optional): Create a small hole in the center of the gelato about 1 1/2 inch deep using a spoon. Add your choice of almonds or walnuts. Select the "Mix-in" program to blend evenly.
5. Re-spin (Optional): For an even creamier texture, you may choose to re-spin the gelato once or twice more.

HEALTH BENEFITS

- Antioxidants: Rich in antioxidants from the berries, which help protect the body against free radicals.

HEALTHY TIPS

- Milk Choices: Use unsweetened or plant-based milk varieties to reduce overall sugar intake.

Nutritional Information (Per Serving): Calories: 200 | Fat: 5g | Carbohydrates: 25g | Protein: 16g

Strawberry Kiwi Protein Swirl

Delight in the fresh and fruity flavors of strawberry and kiwi combined in this Strawberry Kiwi Protein Swirl Gelato. This light and refreshing treat is perfect for a nutritious snack or dessert.

INGREDIENTS:

- 1 cup frozen strawberries
- 1 kiwi, peeled and sliced
- 1/2 cup Greek yogurt
- 1 scoop vanilla protein powder
- Almonds or walnuts (for mix-ins)

Prep Time: 5 minutes Skill Level: Easy

Freezing Time: 24 hours Servings: 2

INSTRUCTIONS

1. In a blender, combine the frozen strawberries, sliced kiwi, Greek yogurt, and protein powder. Blend until smooth.
2. Transfer the blended mixture to a Ninja Creami pint, making sure not to overfill. Freeze for at least 24 hours.
3. Place the frozen pint in the Ninja Creami Deluxe and select the "Gelato" function. Process until creamy.
4. Mix-In (Optional): Create a small hole in the center of the gelato about 1 1/2 inch deep using a spoon. Add almonds or walnuts. Select the "Mix-in" program to blend evenly.
5. Re-spin (Optional): For an even creamier texture, re-spin the gelato once or twice more.

HEALTH BENEFITS

- Vitamin C: Strawberries and kiwi are high in Vitamin C, which is essential for immune health and skin vitality.
- Protein: Supports muscle recovery and satiety thanks to the protein powder.

HEALTHY TIPS

- Fresh Fruit: Using fresh, frozen fruits ensures maximum nutrient retention and flavor.
- Yogurt Selection: Opt for low-fat Greek yogurt to keep calories in check.

Nutritional Information (Per Serving): Calories: 210 | Fat: 6g | Carbohydrates: 22g | Protein: 18g

Fuel your summer adventures with every scoop – power up with flavor, cool down with delight

Stracciatella Protein

Experience the delight of classic Italian ice

Cream with a healthy twist in this Stracciatella Protein Gelato. Featuring fine shards of dark chocolate swirled through creamy gelato; it is a treat that is as satisfying as it is nutritious.

INGREDIENTS

- 1 cup almond milk
- 1/2 cup Greek yogurt
- 1 scoop vanilla protein powder
- 2 tablespoons honey
- 1/4 cup dark chocolate, finely chopped (for mix-ins)

Prep Time: 5 minutes Skill Level: Easy

Freezing Time: 24 hours Servings: 2

INSTRUCTIONS

1. Combine almond milk, Greek yogurt, protein powder, and honey in a blender. Blend until smooth.
2. Transfer the blended mixture to a Ninja Creami pint container. Ensure it does not overfill. Freeze for at least 24 hours.
3. Place the frozen pint in the Ninja Creami Deluxe and select the "Gelato" function. Process until it reaches a creamy texture.
4. Mix-In (Optional): Create a small hole in the center of the gelato about 1 1/2 inch deep using a spoon. Add the finely chopped dark chocolate. Select the "Mix-in" program to evenly distribute the chocolate shards.
5. Re-spin (Optional): Re-spin the gelato once or twice for an extra creamy texture.

HEALTH BENEFITS

- Bone Health: Almond milk and Greek yogurt provide calcium for strong bones.
- Antioxidants: Dark chocolate is rich in antioxidants that help reduce oxidative stress.

HEALTHY TIPS

- Chocolate Selection: Choose high-quality dark chocolate with a cocoa content of at least 70% for maximum health benefits.
- Sweetener Choices: Adjust the sweetness by using natural sweeteners like honey or maple syrup to taste.

Nutritional Information (Per Serving): Calories: 230 | Fat: 9g | Carbohydrates: 24g | Protein: 15g

Tropical Passion Fruit

Immerse yourself in the exotic flavors of the tropics with this Tropical Passion Fruit Protein Gelato. This refreshing treat combines the unique tangy taste of passion fruit with creamy texture and protein benefits, making it a perfect dessert for health-conscious indulgence.

INGREDIENTS

- 1 cup passion fruit pulp (fresh or frozen)
- 1/2 cup coconut milk
- 1 scoop vanilla protein powder
- 2 tablespoons agave syrup
- Shredded coconut (optional, for mix-ins)

Prep Time: 5 minutes Skill Level: Easy

Freezing Time: 24 hours Servings: 2

Equipment:

- Blender, Bowl, Spatula

INSTRUCTIONS

1. In a blender, combine passion fruit pulp, coconut milk, protein powder, and agave syrup. Blend until smooth.
2. Transfer the blended mixture to a Ninja Creami pint container, taking care not to overfill. Freeze for at least 24 hours.
3. Place the frozen pint into the Ninja Creami Deluxe and select the "Gelato" function. Process until the texture becomes creamy.
4. Mix-In (Optional): Create a small hole in the center of the gelato about 1 1/2 inch deep using a spoon. Add shredded coconut. Select the "Mix-in" program to blend evenly.
5. Re-spin (Optional): For an even creamier texture, re-spin the gelato once or twice more.

HEALTH BENEFITS

- Vitamin C: Passion fruit is a rich source of Vitamin C, vital for immune system support and skin health.
- Healthy Fats: Coconut milk provides medium-chain triglycerides (MCTs), which are known for their energy-boosting properties.

HEALTHY TIPS

- Natural Sweeteners: Use agave syrup or another natural sweetener to keep the sugar content lower.
- Coconut Milk: Choose unsweetened coconut milk to minimize added sugars while still enjoying its creamy texture.

Nutritional Information (Per Serving): Calories: 220 | Fat: 8g | Carbohydrates: 26g | Protein: 12g

Vanilla Chai Protein Shake

Savor in the aromatic and comforting flavors of chai with this Vanilla Chai Protein Shake Gelato. This gelato combines the warm spices of chai with vanilla and protein, making it a delightful treat that is both nutritious and satisfying.

INGREDIENTS:

- 1 cup almond milk
- 1/2 cup Greek yogurt
- 1 scoop vanilla protein powder
- 2 tablespoons chai spice mix (cinnamon, cardamom)
- 1 tablespoon honey

Prep Time: 5 minutes Skill Level: Easy

Freezing Time: 24 hours Servings: 2

Equipment

- Blender, Bowl, Spatula

INSTRUCTIONS

1. In a blender, combine almond milk, Greek yogurt, vanilla protein powder, chai spice mix, and honey. Blend until smooth.
2. Transfer the blended mixture to a Ninja Creami pint container, making sure not to overfill. Freeze for at least 24 hours.
3. Insert the frozen pint into the Ninja Creami Deluxe and select the "Gelato" function. Process until the mixture reaches a creamy texture.
4. Mix-In (Optional): Create a small hole in the center of the gelato about 1 1/2 inch

deep using a spoon. Add any additional spices or a swirl of honey. Select the "Mix-in" program to blend evenly.
5. Re-spin (Optional): For a creamier texture, re-spin the gelato once or twice more.

HEALTH BENEFITS

- Digestive Health: The spices in chai, such as ginger and cardamom, are known for their digestive benefits and anti-inflammatory properties.
- Bone Health: Greek yogurt provides calcium and protein, essential for bone health and muscle recovery.

HEALTHY TIPS

Spice Adjustment: Adjust the chai spice mix according to taste preference; you can make it milder or stronger based on your liking.

Nutritional Information (Per Serving): Calories: 180 | Fat: 4g | Carbohydrates: 18g | Protein: 16g

Honey Lavender Protein Gelato

Relax and unwind with the soothing flavors of Honey Lavender Protein Gelato. This delicate and floral dessert combines the calming properties of lavender with the sweetness of honey, all while providing a healthy protein boost.

INGREDIENTS

- 1 cup almond milk
- 1/2 cup Greek yogurt
- 1 scoop vanilla protein powder
- 1 tablespoon dried lavender flowers
- 2 tablespoons honey

Prep Time: 5 minutes Skill Level: Easy

Freezing Time: 24 hours   Servings: 2

Equipment:

- Blender, Bowl, spatula
- Ninja Creami Deluxe

INSTRUCTIONS

1. In a blender, mix almond milk, Greek yogurt, vanilla protein powder, lavender flowers, and honey until smooth.
2. Transfer blended the mixture to a Ninja Creami pint container. Do not overfill. Freeze for at least 24 hours.
3. Place the frozen pint into your Ninja Creami Deluxe and select the "Gelato" function. Process until the texture is creamy.
4. Mix-In (Optional): Create a small hole in the center of the gelato about 1 1/2 inch deep using a spoon. If desired, add a small additional amount of dried lavender for enhanced flavor. Select the "Mix-in" program to incorporate smoothly.
5. Re-spin (Optional): Re-spin the gelato once or twice for an even creamier texture.

HEALTH BENEFITS

- Stress Relief: Lavender is renowned for its ability to reduce stress and promote relaxation.
- Protein Rich: Helps in muscle recovery and provides sustained energy thanks to the protein powder.

HEALTHY TIPS

- Lavender Quality: Use culinary-grade lavender to ensure it is safe for consumption.

Nutritional Information (Per Serving): Calories: 200 | Fat: 5g | Carbohydrates: 22g | Protein: 18g

Protein Powerhouse Pistachio

Enjoy the rich, nutty flavor of pistachios in this Protein Powerhouse Pistachio Gelato. This dessert is not only delicious but also packed with protein and healthy fats, making it a guilt-free treat that is perfect for any time of day.

INGREDIENTS

- 1 cup unsweetened almond milk

- 1/2 cup Greek yogurt
- 1 scoop vanilla protein powder
- 1/4 finely ground pistachios
- 1 tablespoon honey

Prep Time: 5 minutes Skill Level: Easy

Freezing Time: 24 hours Servings: 2

Equipment:

- Blender, Bowl, Spatula
- Ninja Creami Deluxe

INSTRUCTIONS

1. Combine almond milk, Greek yogurt, vanilla protein powder, pistachio paste, and honey in a blender. Blend until smooth.
2. Transfer the blended mixture to a Ninja Creami pint container, ensuring not to overfill. Freeze for at least 24 hours.
3. Place the frozen pint in the Ninja Creami Deluxe and select the "Gelato" function. Process until the texture becomes creamy.
4. Mix-In (Optional): Create a small hole in the center of the gelato about 1 1/2 inch deep using a spoon. Add additional chopped pistachios if desired. Select the "Mix-in" program to blend evenly.
5. Re-spin (Optional): For an even creamier texture, re-spin the gelato once or twice more.

HEALTH BENEFITS

Heart Health: Pistachios are known for their heart-healthy fats and may help in lowering cholesterol.

Protein and Energy: Provides a good source of protein from Greek yogurt and protein powder, which helps in muscle recovery and sustained energy.

HEALTHY TIPS

- Pistachio Selection: Use unsalted pistachio paste or nuts to control sodium intake.

Nutritional Information (Per Serving): Calories: 240 | Fat: 10g | Carbohydrates: 24g | Protein: 15g

Keto Coffee Gelato

Energize your day with this Keto Coffee Gelato, combining the rich taste of coffee with the benefits of a keto-friendly composition. Perfect for those following a low-carb diet, this gelato offers a delicious way to enjoy a frozen treat without the guilt.

INGREDIENTS

- 1 cup unsweetened almond milk
- 1/2 cup heavy cream
- 1 scoop keto-friendly protein powder (vanilla or unflavored)
- 2 tablespoons instant coffee granules
- 1 tablespoon erythritol or preferred keto sweetener

Prep Time: 5 minutes Skill Level: Easy

Freezing Time: 24 hours Servings: 2

Equipment:

- Blender, Spatula, Bowl
- Ninja Creami Deluxe

INSTRUCTIONS

1. Blend: In a blender, mix almond milk, heavy cream, protein powder, instant coffee granules, and erythritol until smooth.
2. Freeze: Transfer the blended mixture into a Ninja Creami pint container, being careful not to overfill. Freeze for at least 24 hours.
3. Gelato Function: Insert the frozen pint into the Ninja Creami Deluxe and select the "Gelato" function. Process until the mixture reaches a creamy texture.
4. Re-spin (Optional): For an extra creamy texture, re-spin the gelato once or twice more.

HEALTH BENEFITS

- Energy Boosting: Coffee is a natural stimulant, providing a quick energy boost.
- Low Carb: Suitable for ketogenic diets, this gelato is low in carbs and high in healthy fats, aiding in ketosis maintenance.

HEALTHY TIPS

- Keto-Friendly Ingredients: Ensure all ingredients are low-carb and keto-approved to maintain ketosis.
- Sweetener Options: Adjust the amount of erythritol or switch to another keto-friendly sweetener based on your taste preference.

Nutritional Information (Per Serving): Calories: 250 | Fat: 22g | Carbohydrates: 5g | Protein: 8g

Hazelnut Chocolate Swirl Protein Gelato

Dig deep in the luxurious blend of hazelnuts and chocolate with this Hazelnut Chocolate Swirl Protein Gelato. This decadent treat is perfect for those looking to enjoy a classic flavor combination while getting a boost of protein.

INGREDIENTS:

- 1 cup unsweetened almond milk
- ½ cup Greek yogurt
- 1 scoop chocolate protein powder
- 2 tablespoons hazelnut butter
- 1/4 cup chopped hazelnuts (for mix-ins)
- 2 tablespoons chocolate syrup (for swirl)

Prep Time: 5 minutes Skill Level: Easy

Freezing Time: 24 hours Servings: 2

Equipment:

- Blender, Bowl, Spatula
- Ninja Creami Deluxe

INSTRUCTIONS

1. In a blender, combine almond milk, Greek yogurt, chocolate protein powder, and hazelnut butter. Blend until smooth.
2. Transfer the blended mixture to a Ninja Creami pint container, careful not to overfill. Freeze for at least 24 hours.
3. Place the frozen pint into the Ninja Creami Deluxe and select the "Gelato" function. Process until the texture becomes creamy.
4. Mix-In: Create a small hole in the center of the gelato about 1 1 /2 inch deep using a spoon. Add chopped hazelnuts and drizzle chocolate syrup. Select the "Mix-in" program to evenly distribute the hazelnuts and create a swirl with the chocolate.
5. Re-spin (Optional): For an even creamier texture, re-spin the gelato once or twice more.

HEALTH BENEFITS

- Heart Health: Hazelnuts are rich in healthy fats, vitamins, and minerals that promote heart health.
- Muscle Recovery: Protein powder helps in muscle recovery and satiety, making this gelato a great post-workout treat.

HEALTHY TIPS

- Hazelnut Butter Selection: Use pure hazelnut butter without added sugars or oils for the healthiest option.

Nutritional Information (Per Serving): Calories: 310 | Fat: 20g | Carbohydrates: 22g | Protein: 18g

Chunky Monkey Protein Gelato

Savor the playful and indulgent flavors of Chunky Monkey Protein Gelato, a delightful mix of bananas, chocolate, and nuts. This protein-packed dessert is perfect for those who enjoy a rich, satisfying treat while also benefiting from healthful ingredients.

INGREDIENTS

- 1 cup frozen banana slices
- 1/2 cup Greek yogurt
- 1 scoop chocolate protein powder
- 2 tablespoons peanut butter
- 2 tablespoons mini dark chocolate chips (for mix-ins)

Prep Time: 5 minutes Skill Level: Easy

Freezing Time: 24 hours   Servings: 2

INSTRUCTIONS

1. In a blender, combine the frozen banana slices, Greek yogurt, chocolate protein powder, and peanut butter. Blend until smooth.
2. Transfer the blended mixture to a Ninja Creami pint container, ensuring not to overfill. Freeze for at least 24 hours.
3. Place the frozen pint in the Ninja Creami Deluxe and select the "Gelato" function. Process until the texture becomes creamy.
4. Mix-In: Create a small hole in the center of the gelato about 1 1/2 inch deep using a spoon. Add chopped walnuts and mini dark chocolate chips. Select the "Mix-in" program to blend evenly.
5. Re-spin (Optional): For an even creamier texture, re-spin the gelato once or twice more.

HEALTH BENEFITS

- Protein-Rich: Great for muscle recovery and sustained energy, thanks to the high protein content from Greek yogurt and protein powder.
- Healthy Fats: Walnuts and peanut butter provide healthy fats that are good for heart health.

HEALTHY TIPS

- Natural Ingredients: Opt for natural, unsweetened peanut butter to avoid added sugars and unhealthy fats.
- Chocolate Choices: Use dark chocolate chips for less sugar and more antioxidants than regular chocolate chips.

Nutritional Information (Per Serving): Calories: 320 | Fat: 18g | Carbohydrates: 28g, Protein 35

"Fuel your adventures with protein-powered recipes."

Tropical Protein Punch Sorbet

Enjoy a refreshing burst of tropical flavors with this Tropical Protein Punch Sorbet. Packed with a mix of tropical fruits and a boost of protein, this sorbet is not only delicious but also helps in muscle recovery and hydration.

INGREDIENTS

- 1 cup frozen pineapple chunks
- 1 cup frozen mango chunks
- 1/2 cup orange juice
- 1 scoop vanilla protein powder
- 1 tablespoon lime juice
- Coconut flakes (optional, for mix-ins)

Preparation Time: 5 minutes Skill Level: Easy

Freezing Time: 24 hours Servings: 2

INSTRUCTIONS

1. Blend: In a blender, combine frozen pineapple, mango chunks, orange juice, vanilla protein powder, and lime juice. Blend until smooth.
2. Freeze: Transfer the blended mixture to a Ninja Creami pint container. Freeze for about 24 hours,
3. Sorbet Function: Place the frozen pint in the Ninja Creami Deluxe and select the "Sorbet" function. Process until the texture becomes creamy.
4. Mix-In (Optional): After the sorbet is partially frozen, create a small hole in the center about 1 1/2 inch deep using a spoon. Add coconut flakes. Use the "Mix-in" program to blend evenly.
5. Serve: Once the sorbet reaches, the desired consistency and the mix-ins are well incorporated, scoop into bowls and serve immediately.

HEALTH BENEFITS

- Tropical fruits like mango and pineapple are naturally rich in electrolytes like potassium and magnesium, which are essential for hydration and muscle function.

HEALTHY TIPS

- Choose Natural Sweeteners like dates or honey to avoid added sugars. This not only enhances the flavor but also keeps the sorbet healthier.

Nutritional Information (Per Serving): Calories: 180 | Fat: 1g | Carbohydrates: 35g | Protein: 10g

Chocolate Peanut Butter Protein Sorbet

Leap into the indulgent and satisfying flavors of chocolate and peanut butter with this Chocolate Peanut Butter Protein Sorbet. It is a fantastic choice for a dessert that combines the creamy texture of peanut butter with the rich taste of chocolate, all while delivering a solid protein punch.

INGREDIENTS

- 1 cup unsweetened almond milk
- 2 tablespoons unsweetened cocoa powder
- 1 scoop chocolate protein powder
- 2 tablespoons natural peanut butter
- 1 tablespoon honey
- Mini chocolate chips (optional, for mix-ins)

Preparation Time: 5 minutes Skill Level: Easy

Freezing Time: 24 hours Servings: 2

INSTRUCTIONS

1. Blend: In a blender, mix almond milk, cocoa powder, chocolate protein powder, peanut butter, and honey until smooth.

2. Freeze: Transfer the blended mixture to a Ninja Creami pint container. Freeze for about 24 hours.

3. Sorbet Function: After freezing, place the mixture in the Ninja Creami Deluxe and select the "Sorbet" function. Process until the texture becomes creamy.

4. Mix-In (Optional): After the sorbet is processed, create a small hole in the center about 1 1/2 inch deep using a spoon. Add mini chocolate chips. Use the "Mix-in" program to blend evenly.

5. Serve: Once the mix-ins are integrated and the sorbet reaches the desired consistency, scoop into bowls and serve immediately.

HEALTH BENEFITS

- Protein: Crucial for muscle repair and growth, metabolism, and satiety.

HEALTHY TIPS

- Choose high-quality cocoa powder, natural peanut butter (without added sugar or oils), and unsweetened milk or yogurt for the base.

Nutritional Information (Per Serving): Calories: 280 | Fat: 16g | Carbohydrates: 25g | Protein: 15g

Berry Vanilla Protein Swirl Sorbet

Enjoy a refreshing and healthful twist on dessert with this Berry Vanilla Protein Swirl Sorbet. Featuring a delicious blend of mixed berries and a hint of vanilla, this sorbet is both protein-packed and full of antioxidant-rich fruits, making it a perfect treat for any time.

INGREDIENTS

- 1 cup frozen mixed berries (strawberries, blueberries, raspberries)
- 1/2 cup water or almond milk
- 1 scoop vanilla protein powder
- 1 tablespoon honey
- Fresh berries (optional, for mix-ins)

Preparation Time: 5 minutes Skill Level: Easy

Freezing Time: 24 hours Servings: 2

INSTRUCTIONS

1. Blend: Combine frozen mixed berries, water or almond milk, vanilla protein powder, and honey in a blender. Blend until smooth.
2. Freeze: Transfer the blended mixture to a Ninja Creami pint container. Freeze for about 24 hours.
3. Sorbet Function: After freezing, place the mixture in the Ninja Creami Deluxe and select the "Sorbet" function. Process until the texture becomes creamy.
4. Mix-In (Optional): Once the sorbet is semi-frozen, create a small hole in the center about 1 1/2 inch deep using a spoon. Add fresh berries. Use the "Mix-in" program to blend evenly.
5. Serve: Once the sorbet reaches, the desired consistency and the mix-ins are well incorporated, scoop into bowls and serve immediately.

HEALTH BENEFITS

- Fiber: Promotes digestive health, regulates blood sugar levels, and aids in weight management.
- Antioxidants: Protect your cells from damage caused by free radicals, contributing to overall health and well-being.

HEALTHY TIPS

- Freeze Fruit: Use frozen berries and bananas for a thicker, creamier consistency.

Nutritional Information (Per Serving): Calories: 180 | Fat: 1g | Carbohydrates: 30g | Protein: 10g

Creamy Coconut Sorbet

Delight in the silky and lush flavors of coconut with this Creamy Coconut Sorbet. Simple and elegant, this sorbet offers a refreshing escape to tropical bliss with each scoop.

INGREDIENTS

- 1 cup coconut milk
- 1/2 cup coconut water
- 2 tablespoons shredded coconut
- 1 tablespoon honey
- Lime zest (optional, for mix-ins)

Preparation Time: 5 minutes Skill Level: Easy

Freezing Time: 24 hours Servings: 2

INSTRUCTIONS

1. Blend: In a blender, combine coconut milk, coconut water, shredded coconut, and honey. Blend until smooth.
2. Freeze Transfer the blended mixture to a Ninja Creami pint container. Freeze for about 24 hours.
3. Sorbet Function: Place the frozen pint in the Ninja Creami Deluxe and select the "Sorbet" function. Process until the texture becomes creamy.
4. Mix-In (Optional): Once the sorbet is semi-frozen, create a small hole in the center about 1 1/2 inch deep using a spoon. Add lime zest. Use the "Mix-in" program to blend evenly.
5. Serve: Once the sorbet reaches, the desired consistency and the mix-ins are well incorporated, scoop into bowls and enjoy immediately.

HEALTH BENEFITS

- Hydration: Coconut water is a natural hydrator, rich in electrolytes, ideal for replenishing body fluids.
- Healthy Fats: Coconut milk provides medium-chain triglycerides (MCTs) which are beneficial for energy production and overall health.

HEALTHY TIPS

- Coconut Choices: Choose unsweetened coconut milk and natural coconut water to minimize added sugars.
- Natural Sweetening: Adjust the level of honey to suit your sweetness preference, or substitute with a natural sweetener like stevia for an even healthier variant.

Nutritional Information (Per Serving): Calories: 200 | Fat: 15g | Carbohydrates: 18g | Protein: 2g

Strawberry Summer Sorbet

Delight in the unique and refreshing blend of sweet strawberries. This strawberry sorbet is perfect for a light dessert or a palate cleanser between courses, this sorbet pairs the natural sweetness of strawberries offering a sophisticated twist on a classic frozen treat.

INGREDIENTS

- 1 cup fresh strawberries, hulled and sliced
- 1/2 cup water
- 1 scoop vanilla protein powder
- 2 tablespoons honey
- A handful of coconut (for mix-ins and)

Preparation Time: 5 minutes Skill Level: Easy

Freezing Time: 24 hours Servings: 2

INSTRUCTIONS

1. Blend: Combine strawberries, water, vanilla protein powder, and honey in a blender. Blend until the mixture is smooth.
2. Freeze: Transfer the blended mixture to a Ninja Creami pint container. Freeze for about 24 hours.
3. Sorbet Function: After freezing, place the mixture in the Ninja Creami Deluxe and select the "Sorbet" function. Process until the texture becomes creamy.
4. Mix-In (Optional): Create a small hole in the center of the sorbet about 1 1/2 inch deep using a spoon. Add fresh basil leaves. Use the "Mix-in" program to blend evenly.
5. Serve: Once the mix-ins are integrated and the sorbet reaches the desired consistency, scoop into bowls, garnish with additional basil if desired, and serve immediately.

HEALTH BENEFITS

- Antioxidants and Vitamin C: Strawberries are a fantastic source of antioxidants and vitamin C, enhancing immune function and skin health.
- Digestive and Anti-inflammatory Benefits: Basil not only enhances flavor but also provides digestive benefits and anti-inflammatory properties.

HEALTHY TIPS

- Protein Boost: Choose a high-quality vanilla protein powder to enrich the sorbet with protein

Nutritional Information (Per Serving):
Calories: 150 | Fat: 0.5g | Carbohydrates: 28g | Protein: 8g

Mango Lassi Sorbet

Transport your taste buds to a tropical paradise with this Mango Lassi Sorbet. Inspired by the traditional Indian drink, this sorbet combines the lush sweetness of ripe mangoes with the tanginess of yogurt, creating a creamy and refreshing dessert that is both indulgent and refreshing.

INGREDIENTS

- 1 cup ripe mango, chopped
- 1/2 cup plain Greek yogurt
- 1 scoop vanilla protein powder
- 2 tablespoons honey
- A pinch of ground cardamom (optional, for mix-in)

Preparation Time: 5 minutes Skill Level: Easy

Freezing Time: 24 hours Servings: 2

INSTRUCTIONS

1. Blend: In a blender, combine chopped mango, Greek yogurt, vanilla protein powder, and honey. Blend until smooth.
2. Freeze: Transfer the blended mixture to a Ninja Creami pint container. Freeze for about 24.
3. Sorbet Function: After freezing, place the mixture in the Ninja Creami Deluxe and select the "Sorbet" function. Process until the texture becomes creamy.
4. Mix-In (Optional): Create a small hole in the center of the sorbet about 1 1/2 inch deep using a spoon. Add a pinch of ground cardamom. Use the "Mix-in" program to blend evenly.
5. Serve: Once the mix-ins are integrated and the sorbet reaches the desired consistency, scoop into bowls and serve immediately.

HEALTH BENEFITS

- Vitamin A and C: Mangoes are a rich source of vitamins A and C, which are essential for immune function and skin health.
- Digestive Health: Greek yogurt provides probiotics that support digestive health.

HEALTHY TIPS

- Spice It Up: Cardamom not only adds a subtle spiced flavor but also aids in digestion and enhances the overall aromatic experience.

Nutritional Information (Per Serving): Calories: 180 | Fat: 1g | Carbohydrates: 33g | Protein: 10g

Protein Blast Berry Mix Sorbet

Invigorate your senses and boost your protein intake with the Protein Blast Berry Mix Sorbet. This delicious sorbet combines a variety of fresh berries for a burst of antioxidants and a scoop of protein powder for muscle support, making it a perfect post-workout treat or a healthy snack.

INGREDIENTS

- 1 cup mixed berries (blueberries, raspberries, blackberries)
- 1/2 cup coconut water
- 1 scoop mixed berry protein powder
- 1 tablespoon agave syrup
- almonds (optional, for mix-ins)

Prep Time: 5 minutes Skill Level: Easy

Freezing Time: 24 hours Servings: 2

INSTRUCTIONS

1. Blend: In a blender, combine mixed berries, coconut water, mixed berry protein powder, and agave syrup. Blend until smooth.
2. Freeze: Transfer the blended mixture to a Ninja Creami pint container. Freeze for about 24 hours.
3. Sorbet Function: After freezing, place the mixture in the Ninja Creami Deluxe and select the "Sorbet" function. Process until the texture becomes creamy.
4. Mix-In (Optional): After the sorbet is processed, create a small hole in the center about 1 1/2 inch deep using a spoon. Add the almonds. Use the "Mix-in" program to blend evenly.
5. Serve: Once the mix-ins are integrated and the sorbet reaches the desired consistency, scoop into bowls and serve immediately.

HEALTH BENEFITS

- Antioxidants: Berries are high in antioxidants, which help reduce inflammation and protect cells from damage.
- Hydration: Coconut water is an excellent source of hydration and electrolytes.

HEALTHY TIPS

- Protein Powder: Choose a protein powder that complements the natural sweetness of the berries without adding artificial flavors.

Nutritional Information (Per Serving): Calories: 180 | Fat: 1g | Carbohydrates: 30g | Protein: 15g

Tropical Protein Paradise Sorbet

Escape to a tropical paradise with every spoonful of this Tropical Protein Paradise

Sorbet. This sorbet melds the flavors of exotic fruits with a boost of protein, creating a refreshing and nutritious treat that is perfect for cooling down on a hot day or refueling after a workout.

INGREDIENTS

- 1 cup frozen pineapple chunks
- 1 cup frozen mango chunks
- 1/2 cup orange juice
- 1 scoop vanilla protein powder
- Shredded coconut (optional, for mix-in)

Preparation Time: 5 minutes Skill Level: Easy

Freezing Time: 24 hours Servings: 2

INSTRUCTIONS

1. Blend: Combine frozen pineapple, mango chunks, orange juice, and vanilla protein powder in a blender. Blend until smooth.
2. Freeze: Transfer the blended mixture to a Ninja Creami pint container. Freeze for about 24 hours.
3. Sorbet Function: After freezing, place the mixture in the Ninja Creami Deluxe and select the "Sorbet" function. Process until the texture becomes creamy.
4. Mix-In (Optional): After the sorbet is processed, create a small hole in the center about 1 1/2 inch deep using a spoon. Add shredded coconut. Use the "Mix-in" program to blend evenly.
5. Serve: Once the mix-ins are integrated and the sorbet reaches the desired consistency, scoop into bowls and serve immediately.

HEALTH BENEFITS

- Vitamin C Boost: Pineapple and mango are loaded with vitamin C, aiding in immune support and skin health.
- Hydration: Orange juice provides additional hydration and a burst of citrus flavor.

HEALTHY TIPS

- Protein Choice: Opt for a high-quality vanilla protein powder that blends well with tropical flavors.

Nutritional Information (Per Serving): Calories: 200 | Fat: 2g | Carbohydrates: 35g | Protein: 12g

Tart Cherry Protein Power Sorbet

Recharge with the Tart Cherry Protein Power Sorbet, featuring the distinctively sharp taste of tart cherries coupled with protein for muscle recovery. Ideal for athletes and those seeking a refreshing, nutritious boost.

INGREDIENTS

- 1 cup tart cherry juice (unsweetened)
- 1 scoop vanilla protein powder
- 1 tablespoon honey
- 1 teaspoon lemon juice
- Dark chocolate shavings (optional, for mix-ins)

Preparation Time: 5 minutes Skill Level: Easy

Freezing Time: 24 hours Servings: 2

INSTRUCTIONS

1. Blend: Mix tart cherry juice, vanilla protein powder, honey, and lemon juice in a blender until smooth.
2. Freeze: Transfer the blended mixture to a Ninja Creami pint container. Freeze for about 24 hours.
3. Sorbet Function: After freezing, place the mixture in the Ninja Creami Deluxe and select the "Sorbet" function. Process until the texture becomes creamy.
4. Mix-In (Optional): After the sorbet is processed, create a small hole in the center about 1 1/2 inch deep using a spoon. Add dark chocolate shavings.

Use the "Mix-in" program to blend evenly.
5. Serve: Once the mix-ins are integrated and the sorbet reaches the desired consistency, scoop into bowls and serve immediately.

HEALTH BENEFITS

- Muscle Recovery: Tart cherry juice is known for its anti-inflammatory properties and can help reduce muscle soreness.
- Antioxidants: High in antioxidants, tart cherries support overall health and can help combat oxidative stress.

HEALTHY TIPS

- Natural Sweeteners: Adjust the sweetness by modifying the amount of honey based on your preference.
- Protein Selection: Use a high-quality protein powder to ensure it blends seamlessly without altering the natural tartness of the cherry juice.

Nutritional Information (Per Serving): Calories: 180 | Fat: 1g | Carbohydrates: 30g | Protein: 10g

Raspberry-Lime Protein Fizz Sorbet

Experience a refreshing burst of citrus and berry flavors with the Raspberry-Lime Protein Fizz Sorbet. This vibrant sorbet combines the tartness of raspberries and the zesty punch of lime, enriched with protein for a nourishing and invigorating frozen treat that is perfect for cooling off on a hot day or summer.

INGREDIENTS

- 1 cup fresh raspberries
- Juice of 2 limes
- ½ cup sparkling water
- 1 scoop lime-flavored protein powder
- 1 tablespoon agave syrup
- Fresh lime zest (optional, for mix-ins)

Preparation Time: 5 minutes Skill Level: Easy

Freezing Time: 24 hours Servings: 2

INSTRUCTIONS

1. Blend: In a blender, combine raspberries, limejuice, sparkling water, lime-flavored protein powder, and agave syrup. Blend until smooth.
2. Freeze: Transfer the blended mixture to a Ninja Creami pint container. Freeze for about 24 hours.
3. Sorbet Function: After freezing, place the mixture in the Ninja Creami Deluxe and select the "Sorbet" function. Process until the texture becomes creamy.
4. Mix-In (Optional): After the sorbet is processed, create a small hole in the center about 1 1/2 inch deep using a spoon. Add fresh lime zest. Use the "Mix-in" program to blend evenly.
5. Serve: Once the mix-ins are integrated and the sorbet reaches the desired consistency, scoop into bowls and serve immediately.

HEALTH BENEFITS

- Raspberries and limes both are rich in vitamin C, which supports immune health and skin vitality.
- Hydration: The inclusion of sparkling water adds a unique fizz and helps maintain hydration.

HEALTHY TIPS

- Protein Powder Choice: Use a high-quality lime-flavored protein powder to complement the citrus notes of the sorbet.

Nutritional Information (Per Serving): Calories: 160 | Fat: 1g | Carbohydrates: 25g | Protein: 12g

Citrus Sunshine protein Lite Ice

Brighten up your day with the Citrus Sunshine Lite Ice Protein Sorbet. This sorbet blends the vibrant flavors of various citrus fruits with a light and refreshing texture, enhanced with protein for a nourishing boost. It is a perfect treat to enjoy any time you need a burst of sunshine.

INGREDIENTS

- 1 cup mixed citrus fruits (orange, grapefruit, lemon)
- Juice of 1 lime
- 1 scoop vanilla protein powder
- 1 tablespoon honey
- Orange zest (optional, for mix-ins)

Prep Time: 5 Minutes Skill Level: Easy

Freezing Time: 24 Hours Servings: 2

INSTRUCTIONS

1. Blend: In a blender, combine mixed citrus fruits, limejuice, vanilla protein powder, and honey. Blend until smooth.
2. Freeze: Transfer the blended mixture to a Ninja Creami pint container. Freeze for about 24 hours.
3. Lite Ice Function: After freezing, place the mixture in the Ninja Creami Deluxe and select the "Lite Ice" function. Process until the texture becomes creamy.
4. Mix-In (Optional): After the lite ice processing, create a small hole in the center about 1 1/2 inch deep using a spoon. Add orange zest. Use the "Mix-in" program to blend evenly.
5. Serve: Once the mix-ins are integrated and the sorbet reaches the desired consistency, scoop into bowls and serve immediately.

HEALTH BENEFITS

- Vitamin C Boost: Rich in vitamin C, the mixed citrus fruits support immune function and promote skin health.
- Hydration: The water content helps maintain hydration, especially beneficial on hot days.

HEALTHY TIPS

- Protein Selection: Choose a high-quality vanilla protein powder that complements the fresh, tangy flavors of the citrus.

Nutritional Information (Per Serving): Calories: 150 | Fat: 1g | Carbohydrates: 22g | Protein: 12g

Salted Caramel Mocha Protein Lite Ice Protein

Indulge in the decadent flavors of coffee and caramel with a hint of salt in this Salted Caramel Mocha Lite Ice Protein Sorbet. This sorbet is a luxurious blend that satisfies coffee lovers and sweet tooths alike, with the added benefit of protein for a healthful twist.

INGREDIENTS

- 1 cup cold brew coffee
- 1/2 cup almond milk
- 1 scoop chocolate protein powder
- 2 tablespoons caramel sauce
- A pinch of sea salt
- Chocolate shavings (optional, for mix-ins)

Prep Time: 5 Minutes Skill Level: Easy

Freezing Time: 24 Hours Servings: 2

INSTRUCTIONS

1. Blend: Mix cold brew coffee, almond milk, chocolate protein powder, caramel sauce, and a pinch of sea salt in a blender until smooth.
2. Freeze: Transfer the blended mixture to a Ninja Creami pint container. Freeze for about 24 hours.
3. Lite Ice Function: After freezing, place the mixture in the Ninja Creami Deluxe and select the "Lite Ice" function. Process until the texture becomes creamy.
4. Mix-In (Optional): After processing, create a small hole in the center about 1 1/2 inch deep using a spoon. Add chocolate shavings. Use the "Mix-in" program to blend evenly.
5. Serve: Once the mix-ins are well incorporated and the sorbet reaches the desired creamy consistency, scoop into bowls and serve immediately.

HEALTH BENEFITS

- Energy Boosting: Coffee is a natural stimulant, providing a quick energy boost.
- Muscle Recovery: Protein powder aids in muscle repair, making this a great post-exercise treat.

HEALTHY TIPS

- Quality Ingredients: Use high-quality caramel and fresh cold brew for the best flavor experience.

Nutritional Information (Per Serving): Calories: 180 | Fat: 3g | Carbohydrates: 25g | Protein: 15g

Matcha Coconut Cream Protein Lite Ice

Savor the subtle, earthy tones of matcha paired with the creamy sweetness of coconut in this Matcha Coconut Cream Lite Ice Protein Sorbet. This refreshing sorbet combines the antioxidant benefits of matcha green tea with the tropical flavors of coconut, creating a healthful energizing afternoon treat.

INGREDIENTS

- 1 cup coconut milk
- 2 teaspoons matcha green tea powder
- 1/2 cup Greek yogurt
- 1 scoop vanilla protein powder
- 1 tablespoon honey
- Shredded coconut (optional, for mix-ins)

Prep Time: 5 Minutes Skill Level: Easy

Freezing Time: 24 Hours Servings: 2

INSTRUCTIONS

1. Combine coconut milk, matcha green tea powder, Greek yogurt, vanilla protein powder, and honey in a blender. Blend until the mixture is smooth and evenly colored.
2. Transfer the blended mixture to a Ninja Creami pint container. Freeze for about 24 hours.
3. Place the frozen mixture into the Ninja Creami Deluxe and select the "Lite Ice" function. Process until the sorbet achieves a creamy, smooth texture.
4. Mix-In (Optional): After processing, create a small hole in the center of the sorbet about 1 1/2 inch deep using a spoon. Add shredded coconut. Use the "Mix-in" program to ensure the coconut is evenly distributed throughout the sorbet.
5. Serve: Once the sorbet is ready and the mix-ins are well incorporated, scoop it into bowls and enjoy immediately.

HEALTH BENEFITS

- Coconut milk provides a source of medium-chain providing a quick source of energy and potentially aiding in weight management.

HEALTHY TIPS

- Matcha Quality: Opt for high quality, ceremonial-grade matcha to get the most health benefits and the best flavor.

Nutritional Information (Per Serving): Calories: 180 | Fat: 8g | Carbohydrates: 15g | Protein: 10g

Tropical Piña Colada Protein Lite Ice

Escape to a tropical paradise with this Tropical Piña Colada Lite Ice Protein Sorbet. This refreshing sorbet combines the classic flavors of pineapple and coconut with a protein boost, making it a perfect treat to enjoy while soaking up the sun or after a workout.

INGREDIENTS

- 1 cup frozen pineapple chunks
- 1/2 cup coconut milk
- 1 scoop vanilla protein powder
- 2 tablespoons shredded coconut
- Pineapple slices (optional, for mix-ins)

Prep Time: 5 Minutes Skill Level: Easy

Freezing Time: 24 Hours Servings: 2

INSTRUCTIONS

1. Blend: In a blender, combine frozen pineapple chunks, coconut milk, vanilla protein powder, and shredded coconut. Blend until smooth.
2. Freeze: Transfer the blended mixture to a Ninja Creami pint container. Freeze for about 24 hours.
3. Lite Ice Function: After freezing, place the mixture in the Ninja Creami Deluxe and select the "Lite Ice" function. Process until the texture becomes creamy.
4. Mix-In (Optional): After processing, create a small hole in the center about 1 1/2 inch deep using a spoon. Add additional pineapple slices. Use the "Mix-in" program to blend evenly.
5. Serve: Once the mix-ins are integrated and the sorbet reaches the desired consistency, scoop into bowls and enjoy the tropical flavors.

HEALTH BENEFITS

- Vitamin C: Pineapple is rich in vitamin C, which is essential for immune system support and skin health.

HEALTHY TIPS

- Protein Source: Select a high-quality vanilla protein powder to enhance the nutritional value without overpowering the natural tropical flavors.
- Coconut Selection: Use unsweetened coconut milk and shredded coconut to keep the sugar content lower.

Nutritional Information (Per Serving):
Calories: 200 | Fat: 8g | Carbohydrates: 25g | Protein: 10g

Low Carb Mint Madness Protein Lite Ice

Enjoy the refreshing burst of mint with the Low Carb Mint Madness Lite Ice. Crafted for those watching their carb intake; this dessert combines the cool flavor of mint with a smooth, light texture, making it a perfect guilt-free indulgence.

INGREDIENTS

- 1 cup heavy cream
- 1/2 cup unsweetened almond milk
- 1 scoop vanilla protein powder
- 2 tablespoons erythritol (or another low-carb sweetener)
- 1 teaspoon mint extract
- Dark chocolate shavings (optional, for mix-ins)

Prep Time: 5 Minutes Skill Level: Easy

Freezing Time: 24 Hours Servings: 2

INSTRUCTIONS

1. In a blender, combine heavy cream, almond milk, vanilla protein powder, erythritol, mint extract, and food coloring if desired. Blend until smooth.
2. Freeze Transfer the blended mixture to a Ninja Creami pint container. Freeze for about 24 hours.
3. Lite Ice Function: After freezing, place the mixture in the Ninja Creami Deluxe and select the "Lite Ice" function. Process until the consistency is creamy.
4. Mix-In (Optional): Create a small hole in the center of the lite ice about 1 1/2 inch deep using a spoon. Add dark chocolate shavings to enhance the mint flavor with a chocolatey twist. Use the "Mix-in" program to blend evenly.
5. Serve: Once the chocolate is well incorporated and the lite ice reaches the desired consistency, scoop into bowls and enjoy this minty treat.

HEALTH BENEFITS

- Low Carb: This lite ice is ideal for keto and other low-carb diets, helping you stay in ketosis while enjoying a delicious treat.
- Protein Boost: Adds a protein kick for muscle maintenance and satiety.

HEALTHY TIPS

- Natural Ingredients: Using natural mint extract ensures a clean, refreshing flavor without artificial additives.

Nutritional Information (Per Serving): Calories: 250 | Fat: 22g | Carbohydrates: 5g | Protein: 8g

Low-Calorie Brownie Chunk Protein Lite Ice

A healthier take on the classic brownie ice cream, delivering rich chocolate flavor with protein and less guilt.

INGREDIENTS

- 1 cup unsweetened almond milk
- 1 scoop chocolate protein powder
- 1/4 cup unsweetened cocoa powder
- 2 tablespoons sweetener of your choice (e.g., stevia, monk fruit)
- 1/4 cup low-fat Greek yogurt
- 1/4 cup crumbled low-calorie brownies

Prep Time: 5-10 Minutes Skill Level: Easy

Freezing Time: 24 Hours Servings: 2

INSTRUCTION

1. Blend: Combine the almond milk, protein powder, cocoa powder, sweetener, and Greek yogurt in a blender. Blend until smooth.
2. Freeze: Transfer the blended mixture to a Ninja Creami pint container. Freeze for about 24 hours.
3. Process: Place the frozen pint in your Ninja Creami Deluxe and select the "Lite Ice Cream" function.
4. Mix-In (Optional): Create a small hole in the center of the lite ice cream about 1 1/2 inches deep using a spoon. Add the crumbled low-calorie brownies and use the "Mix-in" program to blend evenly.
5. Re-Spin: For a creamier texture, re-spin once or twice.

HEALTH BENEFITS

- Lower in calories and fat than traditional brownie ice cream.
- Offers a good source of protein for satiety and muscle repair.
- Can be customized with gluten-free or vegan brownie options.

HEALTHY TIPS

- Choose a protein powder and brownies with minimal added sugar for optimal health benefits.
- If you are not strictly low-calorie, you can use regular milk and full-fat Greek yogurt for a richer texture.

Nutritional Information (Per Serving): Calories: 150 | Fat: 5-7g | Carbs: 15-20g | Protein: 15-18g

Vegan Vanilla Protein Base

A versatile, dairy-free base for countless protein-rich ice cream creations.

INGREDIENTS

- 1 cup of unsweetened almond milk or oat milk
- 1 scoop vanilla plant-based protein powder
- 1/4 cup of maple syrup or agave nectar (adjust to suit your taste)
- 1/4 teaspoon vanilla extract

Prep Time: 5 Minutes Skill Level: Easy

Freezing Time: 24 Hours Servings: 2

INSTRUCTIONS

- Blend: Combine all ingredients in a blender and blend until the mixture is smooth.
- Freeze: Transfer the blended mixture to a Ninja Creami pint container. Freeze for about 24 hours.
- Process: Place the frozen pint in your Ninja Creami Deluxe and select the "Lite Ice Cream" function.
- Mix-In (Optional): Create a small hole in the center of the lite ice cream about 1 1/2 inches deep using a spoon. Add your desired mix-ins (fresh or frozen fruit, chocolate chips, nut butters, or your favorite spices) and use the "Mix-in" program to blend evenly.
- Re-Spin: Re-spin once or twice for a creamier consistency.

HEALTH BENEFITS

- Dairy-free and vegan-friendly.
- Good source of plant-based protein.

HEALTHY TIPS:

- Choose a high-quality plant-based protein powder with minimal additives.
- Experiment with different sweeteners and flavor extracts.

Nutritional Information (Per Serving): Calories: 160 Fat: 8g Carbs: 20g Protein: 18g

NOTE:_____

_____

_____

_____

_____

_____

_____

_____

_____

_____

_____

Protein Coffee Lite Ice Cream

A light and refreshing coffee-flavored treat that delivers a caffeine and protein boost.

INGREDIENTS

- 1 cup cold brew coffee or strongly brewed coffee, chilled
- 1/2 cup milk of choice
- 1 scoop vanilla or mocha protein powder
- 1-2 tablespoons sweetener of your choice (optional)

Prep Time: 5 Minutes Skill Level: Easy

Freezing Time: 24 Hours Servings: 2

INSTRUCTION

1. Combine chilled coffee, milk, protein powder, and sweetener (if using) in a blender. Blend until smooth.
2. Transfer the blended mixture to a Ninja Creami pint container. Freeze for about 24 hours.
3. Place the frozen pint in your Ninja Creami Deluxe and select the "Lite Ice Cream" function.
4. Mix-In (Optional): Create a small hole in the center of the lite ice cream about 1 1/2 inches deep using a spoon. Add your desired mix-ins (e.g., a sprinkle of cocoa powder or a few chocolate chips) and use the "Mix-in" program to blend evenly.
5. Re-Spin: Re-spin once or twice for a creamier consistency.

HEALTH BENEFITS

- Provides a boost of caffeine for energy and alertness.
- Offers a good source of protein for satiety and muscle repair.

HEALTHY TIPS

- Use unsweetened milk or a plant-based alternative for a lower-calorie option.

Nutritional Information (Per Serving): Calories: 140-| Fat: 4-6g | Carbs: 10-15g | Protein: 15-18g

"Ninja Creami Lite ice cream offers a guilt-free, refreshing treat perfect for beating the summer heat and satisfying your sweet cravings."

Greek Yogurt Protein Base

Create a foundational component for your nutritious recipes with the Greek Yogurt Protein Base. This recipe blends the thick, creamy consistency of Greek yogurt with added protein, making it perfect for those seeking a versatile and healthy base for various culinary creations.

INGREDIENTS

- 2 cups plain Greek yogurt
- 1 scoop vanilla or unflavored protein powder
- 1 tablespoon honey or maple syrup (optional, for sweetness)

Prep Time: 5 minutes Skill Level: Easy

Freezing Time: 24 hours Servings: 2

INSTRUCTIONS

- Mix Ingredients: In a mixing bowl, combine the Greek yogurt, protein powder, and honey or maple syrup. Combine thoroughly until all the ingredients are well integrated.
- Freeze: Transfer the mixture to a Ninja Creami pint container. Freeze for at least 24 hours to ensure it solidifies properly.
- Yogurt Function: Place the frozen pint in your Ninja Creami Deluxe and select the "Yogurt" function. Process until it reaches a soft-serve consistency.
- Mix-In (Optional): Create a small hole in the center of the yogurt about 1 1/2 inch deep using a spoon. Add any desired mix-ins, such as nuts or fruit pieces. Use the "Mix-in" program to incorporate them evenly throughout the yogurt.
- Re-spin (Optional): For a firmer texture, especially after adding mix-ins, select the "Yogurt" program again to reprocess.

HEALTH BENEFITS

- High Protein: Supports muscle repair and growth, ideal for those with active lifestyles.
- Digestive Health: The probiotics in Greek yogurt help maintain a healthy digestive system and boost immunity.

HEALTHY TIPS

- Protein Powder Choices: Select a protein powder that complements the natural tanginess of the yogurt or one that enhances the overall flavor profile.

Nutritional Information (Per Serving): Calories: 190 | Fat: 4g | Carbohydrates: 12g | Protein: 28g

Tropical Protein Yogurt Delight

Transport yourself to a tropical paradise with every spoonful of this Tropical Protein Yogurt Delight. Infused with the flavors of exotic fruits and enriched with protein, this yogurt dish is both a delightful treat and a nutritious powerhouse, perfect for starting your day or as a refreshing snack.

INGREDIENTS

- 1 cup Greek yogurt
- 1/2 cup chopped mango
- 1/2 cup chopped pineapple
- 1 scoop vanilla protein powder
- 1 tablespoon coconut flakes
- 1 tablespoon honey (optional, for sweetness)

Prep Time: 5 minutes Skill Level: Easy

Freezing Time: 24 hours Servings: 2

INSTRUCTIONS

1. Mix Ingredients: In a mixing bowl, combine Greek yogurt, chopped mango, chopped pineapple, vanilla protein powder, coconut flakes, and honey if using. Stir thoroughly until all ingredients are well blended.
2. Freeze: Transfer the blended mixture to a Ninja Creami pint container. Freeze for at least 24 hours to ensure it solidifies properly.
3. Yogurt Function: Place the frozen pint in your Ninja Creami Deluxe and select the "Yogurt" function. Process until it reaches a creamy consistency.
4. Mix-In (Optional): Create a small hole in the center of the yogurt about 1 1/2 inch deep using a spoon. Add additional coconut flakes or fresh fruit pieces. Use the "Mix-in" program to incorporate them evenly.
5. Serve: Once the yogurt is creamy and the mix-ins are well incorporated, scoop into bowls and garnish with a sprinkle of coconut flakes or fresh fruit.

HEALTH BENEFITS

- Vitamin C: Mango and pineapple are rich in Vitamin C, which is essential for immune health and skin vitality.
- Protein Boost: Provides a substantial amount of protein from Greek yogurt and protein powder, aiding in muscle repair and satiety.

HEALTHY TIPS

- Fruit Variations: Feel free to mix in other tropical fruits like papaya or kiwi to vary the flavor profile and add more nutritional benefits.

Nutritional Information (Per Serving): Calories: 220 | Fat: 4g | Carbohydrates: 30g | Protein: 20g

Peach Melba Swirl

Dig deep in the sweet and tangy flavors of the Peach Peach Melba Swirl, a delightful combination of peaches, raspberries, and Greek yogurt. This creamy treat is not only visually appealing with its vibrant swirls but also packs a nutritious punch with added protein, making it an excellent choice for a refreshing snack or dessert.

INGREDIENTS

- 1 cup Greek yogurt
- 1 cup fresh peaches, sliced
- 1/2 cup raspberries
- 1 scoop vanilla protein powder
- 2 tablespoons honey
- A few raspberries and mint leaves (optional, for garnish)

Prep Time: 5 minutes Skill Level: Easy

Freezing Time: 24 hours Servings: 2

INSTRUCTIONS

- Blend: In a blender, mix Greek yogurt, sliced peaches, raspberries, vanilla protein powder, and honey. Blend until the mixture is smooth and the fruit is fully incorporated.
- Freeze: Transfer the blended mixture into a Ninja Creami pint container. Freeze for at least 24 hours to ensure it solidifies properly.
- Yogurt Function: Place the frozen pint in your Ninja Creami Deluxe and select the "Yogurt" function. Process until it achieves a creamy, soft-serve consistency.
- Mix-In (Optional): Create a small hole in the center of the yogurt about 1 1/2 inch deep using a spoon. You can add more fresh raspberries or peach slices for added texture and flavor. Use the "Mix-in" program to incorporate them evenly.
- Serve: Once the mix-ins are well integrated and the yogurt reaches the desired consistency, scoop into bowls and garnish with fresh raspberries and mint leaves.

HEALTH BENEFITS

- Antioxidants: Raspberries and peaches are high in antioxidants, which help fight free radicals and support overall health.
- The Greek yogurt base provides a good source of protein and probiotics, which are beneficial for muscle repair and digestive health.

HEALTHY TIPS

- Seasonal Fruit: Use fresh, in-season peaches for the best flavor and nutritional value.

Nutritional Information (Per Serving): Calories: 250 | Fat: 2g | Carbohydrates: 35g | Protein: 25g

High-Protein Parfait

Start your day strong or fuel up mid-afternoon with this High-Protein Parfait. Layering rich Greek yogurt enhanced with protein powder, fresh mixed berries, and crunchy granola, this parfait is not only a treat for your taste buds but also a nutritional powerhouse, perfect for a sustained energy boost.

INGREDIENTS

- 1 cup Greek yogurt
- 1 scoop vanilla protein powder
- 1/2 cup mixed berries (strawberries, blueberries, raspberries)
- 1 tablespoon honey
- 1/4 cup granola
- 1 tablespoon chia seeds (optional, for added texture and nutrients)
- 1 tablespoon chopped nuts (optional, for added crunch)

Prep Time: 5 minutes Skill Level: Easy

Freezing Time: 24 hours Servings: 2

INSTRUCTIONS

1. Mix Ingredients: In a bowl, thoroughly combine Greek yogurt, vanilla protein powder, and honey until smooth.

2. Freeze: Pour the yogurt mixture into a Ninja Creami pint container. Freeze for at least 24 hours to ensure it solidifies properly.

3. Yogurt Function: After freezing, insert the pint into your Ninja Creami Deluxe and select the "Yogurt" function. Process until the mixture achieves a creamy, soft-serve consistency.

4. Mix-In (Optional): For added texture and nutrients, create a small hole in the center of the yogurt about 1 1/2 inch deep using a spoon. Add chia seeds and chopped nuts. Use the "Mix-in" program to incorporate evenly.

5. Assemble and Serve Layer the creamy yogurt with fresh berries and granola in a serving glass or bowl. Enjoy this delightful parfait immediately for a refreshing and filling snack or breakfast.

HEALTH BENEFITS

- Protein Rich: Supports muscle maintenance and growth, while also aiding in feeling full longer.
- Fiber and Antioxidants: Berries and chia seeds provide dietary fiber and antioxidants, which contribute to digestive health and cellular protection.

HEALTHY TIPS

- Diverse Toppings: Customize your parfait with a variety of fruits, seeds, and nuts to enjoy different flavors and textures.

Nutritional Information (Per Serving): Calories: 320 | Fat: 10g | Carbohydrates: 38g | Protein: 28g

Berry Banana Protein Yogurt Delight

The Berry Banana Protein Yogurt Delight combines the natural sweetness of bananas with the tang of mixed berries, all folded into a creamy protein-rich Greek yogurt base. This delightful concoction is perfect for a nutritious breakfast or a satisfying snack.

INGREDIENTS

- 1 cup Greek yogurt
- 1 ripe banana, sliced
- 1/2 cup mixed berries (blueberries, raspberries, strawberries)
- 1 scoop vanilla protein powder
- 1 tablespoon honey
- Additional berries for topping (optional)

Prep Time: 5 minutes Skill Level: Easy

Freezing Time: 24 hours Servings: 2

INSTRUCTIONS

1. Mix Ingredients: In a blender, combine Greek yogurt, sliced banana, mixed berries, vanilla protein powder, and honey. Blend until the mixture is smooth.
2. Freeze: Transfer the blended mixture to a Ninja Creami pint container. Freeze for at least 24 hours to ensure proper solidification.
3. Yogurt Function: After freezing, place the container in your Ninja Creami Deluxe and select the "Yogurt" function. Process until the mixture achieves a creamy, smooth consistency.
4. Mix-In (Optional): Create a small hole in the center of the yogurt about 1 1/2 inch deep using a spoon. Add additional fresh berries if desired. Use the "Mix-in" program to incorporate evenly.
5. Re-spin (Optional): If a firmer texture is desired, especially after adding mix-ins,

select the "Yogurt" program again to reprocess.

6. Serve: Once the yogurt is creamy and the mix-ins are well incorporated, scoop into bowls and garnish with more berries. Enjoy this berrylicious treat fresh and chilled.

HEALTH BENEFITS

- Protein Boost: Ideal for muscle recovery and maintaining satiety throughout the day.
- Antioxidants and Vitamins: Berries and bananas are rich in antioxidants, vitamins, and dietary fiber, supporting overall health and digestion.

HEALTHY TIPS

- Natural Sweeteners: Adjust the level of honey to suit your taste, or substitute it with another natural sweetener such as maple syrup or agave nectar.
- Variety of Berries: Mix and match different types of berries to enhance the nutritional value and flavor profile of the yogurt.

Nutritional Information (Per Serving): Calories: 280 | Fat: 4g | Carbohydrates: 42g | Protein: 20g

Probiotic Protein Boost

Energize your day with the Probiotic Protein Boost, a powerful combination of Greek yogurt enriched with extra protein and probiotics. This nutritious concoction is designed to support your digestive health while providing a solid protein foundation for muscle maintenance and overall wellness.

INGREDIENTS

- 1 cup Greek yogurt
- 1 scoop probiotic protein powder
- 1 tablespoon of honey or agave syrup (optional, for sweetness)
- 1/4 cup your choice of fruits (like kiwi or berries, optional for mix-ins)

Prep Time: 5 minutes Skill Level: Easy

Freezing Time: 24 hours Servings: 2

INSTRUCTIONS

1. Mix Ingredients: In a blender, blend the Greek yogurt, probiotic protein powder, and honey or agave syrup until smooth.
2. Freeze: Transfer the mixture to a Ninja Creami pint container. Freeze for at least 24 hours to ensure it solidifies properly.
3. Yogurt Function: After freezing, place the container in your Ninja Creami Deluxe and select the "Yogurt" function.

Process until the mixture achieves a creamy, smooth consistency.

4. Mix-In (Optional): Create a small hole in the center of the yogurt about 1 1/2 inch deep using a spoon. Add your choice of fruits for added flavor and nutrients. Use the "Mix-in" program to blend evenly.

5. Re-spin (Optional): If a firmer texture is desired, especially after adding mix-ins, select the "Yogurt" program again to reprocess.

6. Serve: Once the mix-ins are well incorporated and the yogurt reaches the desired consistency, scoop into bowls. Enjoy this protein-packed, probiotic-rich treat as a refreshing snack or part of a healthy breakfast.

HEALTH BENEFITS

- Digestive Health: The probiotics in the yogurt and protein powder aid in maintaining a healthy gut flora, improving digestion and immune function.

- Protein Enrichment: Provides a significant boost in protein, supporting muscle repair and growth, and promoting long-lasting satiety.

HEALTHY TIPS

- Customizable Sweetness: Adjust the sweetness according to your preference or dietary needs by modifying the amount of honey or agave syrup.

- Fruit Variations: Add a variety of fruits for mix-in to enhance the nutritional value and introduce different flavors and textures.

Nutritional Information (Per Serving): Calories: 220 | Fat: 4g | Carbohydrates: 20g | Protein: 28g

Green Protein Fro-Yo

Refresh and refuel with the Green Protein Fro-Yo, a deliciously creamy frozen yogurt that combines the nutritional power of green vegetables and protein. This treat is perfect for those looking to enjoy a healthy dessert that does not compromise on taste or texture.

INGREDIENTS

- 1 cup Greek yogurt
- 1 scoop vanilla protein powder
- 1/2 cup spinach or kale, fresh or frozen
- 1 small banana
- 1 tablespoon of honey or agave syrup (Adjust to your sweetness level, is optional)
- 1 tablespoon chia seeds (optional, for mix-ins)

Prep Time: 5 minutes Skill Level: Easy

Freezing Time: 24 hours Servings: 2

INSTRUCTIONS

1. Mix Ingredients: In a blender, combine Greek yogurt, protein powder, spinach or kale, banana, and honey or agave syrup. Blend until the mixture is smooth and evenly green.

2. Freeze: Transfer the blended mixture to a Ninja Creami pint container. Freeze for at least 24 hours to ensure it solidifies properly.

3. Yogurt Function: Place the frozen pint in your Ninja Creami Deluxe and select the "Yogurt" function. Process until the texture becomes creamy.

4. Mix-In (Optional): After processing, create a small hole in the center of the fro-yo about 1 1/2 inch deep using a spoon. Add chia seeds for added texture and nutritional boost. Use the "Mix-in" program to incorporate evenly.

5. Re-spin (Optional): If a firmer texture is desired, especially after adding mix-ins, select the "Yogurt" program again to reprocess.

6. Serve: Once the fro-yo is creamy and the mix-ins are well incorporated, scoop into bowls. This green protein fro-yo is perfect as a revitalizing snack or a nutritious dessert.

HEALTH BENEFITS

- Nutrient-Dense: Packed with vitamins from green vegetables and protein, this fro-yo supports overall health, muscle repair, and energy levels.

- Fiber Boost: Chia seeds add a fiber boost, promoting digestive health and satiety.

HEALTHY TIPS

- Variety of Greens: Experiment with different greens like kale or spinach to find your favorite taste and maximize health benefits.

Nutritional Information (Per Serving): Calories: 240 | Fat: 3g | Carbohydrates: 32g | Protein: 20g

NOTE:_____
_____
_____
_____
_____
_____
_____
_____

Berry Banana Protein Yogurt Delight

A delicious blend of berries and banana with a protein boost for a satisfying and healthy treat.

INGREDIENTS

- 1 cup Greek Yogurt Protein Base (from previous recipes)
- 1/2 cup frozen mixed berries
- 1/2 banana, sliced
- 1/4 cup milk of choice

Prep Time: 5 minutes Skill Level: Easy

Freezing Time: 24 Servings: 2

INSTRUCTIONS

- Combine the Greek Yogurt Protein Base, frozen berries, banana slices, and milk in a blender. Blend until smooth.
- Pour the mixture into a Ninja Creami pint, ensuring it does not go above the max fill line.
- Freeze for at least 24 hours, or until completely frozen solid.
- Place the frozen pint in your Ninja Creami Deluxe and select the "Frozen Yogurt" function.
- Once the processing is complete, you can enjoy your frozen yogurt immediately as a soft-serve or use the "Re-spin" function for a firmer texture.

HEALTH BENEFITS

- High in antioxidants from the berries.
- Good source of potassium and fiber from the banana.
- Provides a large amount of protein, which aids muscle growth and repair.

HEALTHY TIPS

- Use unsweetened almond milk or another milk alternative for a dairy-free option.
- Add a handful of spinach or kale for a boost of greens and additional nutrients.
- Mix-In Tips:Top with your favorite granola, nuts, or seeds for added crunch and flavor.

Nutritional Information (Per Serving):
Calories: 220 | Fat: 5g | Carbs: 30g | Protein: 18g

"Fuel your inner ninja with creamy protein-packed recipes!

Conquer cravings with delicious, guilt-free treats."

Dragon Fruit Protein Delight

A vibrant pink treat that is a refreshing and exotic way to cool down and fuel your muscles. The subtle sweetness of dragon fruit pairs perfectly with a hint of lime for a tropical twist, while the protein powder adds a nutritional boost.

INGREDIENTS

- 1 cup dragon fruit, peeled and diced
- 1/2 cup coconut water
- 1 scoop vanilla protein powder
- 1 tablespoon lime juice
- 1 tablespoon honey (optional,)
- Shredded coconut (optional, for mix-ins)

Prep Time: 5 minutes Skill Level: Easy

Freezing Time: 24 hours Servings: 2

INSTRUCTIONS

1. Blend: In a blender, combine the dragon fruit, coconut water, vanilla protein powder, limejuice, and honey. Blend until smooth.
2. Freeze: Transfer the blended mixture into a Ninja Creami pint container. Freeze for at least 24 hours to ensure it solidifies properly.
3. Place the frozen pint in your Ninja Creami Deluxe and select the "Italian Ice" function. Process until the texture becomes smooth and similar to sorbet.
4. Mix-In (Optional): After processing, create a small hole in the center of the Italian ice about 1 1/2 inch deep using a spoon. Add fresh mint leaves or shredded coconut. Use the "Mix-in" program to incorporate them evenly.
5. Once the mix-ins are well integrated and the Italian ice reaches the desired consistency, scoop into bowls and enjoy this exotic, protein-packed refreshment.

HEALTH BENEFITS

- Coconut water is an excellent source of hydration, perfect for replenishing fluids after exercise.

HEALTHY TIPS

- Ensure the protein powder used is of high quality and blends well with tropical flavors without overpowering them.

Nutritional Information (Per Serving): Calories: 180 | Fat: 1g | Carbohydrates: 25g | Protein: 15g

Strawberry Lemonade Protein Fusion

This sweet and tangy treat is a delightful way to enjoy the classic flavors of strawberry lemonade with a protein boost for a refreshing and healthy dessert.

INGREDIENTS

- 1 cup fresh strawberries, sliced
- Juice of 2 lemons
- 1 scoop lemon or unflavored protein powder
- 1 tablespoon honey (optional,)
- or sliced strawberries (for mix-ins)

Prep Time: 5 minutes Skill Level: Easy

Freezing Time: 24 hours Servings: 2

INSTRUCTIONS

1. In a blender, combine strawberries, lemon juice, water, protein powder, and honey. Blend until the mixture is smooth.
2. Transfer the mixture into a Ninja Creami pint container. Freeze for at least 24 hours to ensure it solidifies properly.
3. Place the frozen pint in your Ninja Creami Deluxe and select the "Italian Ice" function. Process until the texture becomes smooth and resembles traditional Italian ice.
4. Re-spin (Optional): For an even smoother texture, especially if the texture seems too icy, select the "Italian Ice" function again to reprocess.
5. Mix-In (Optional): After the re-spin, create a small hole in the center of the Italian ice about 1 1/2 inch deep using a spoon. Add lemon zest or additional sliced strawberries for enhanced flavor and visual appeal. Use the "Mix-in" program to incorporate them evenly.

HEALTH BENEFITS

- Strawberries and lemons are both rich in Vitamin C, which is essential for immune system support and skin health.

HEALTHY TIPS

- Choose a high-quality protein powder that complements the citrus flavor without overwhelming the natural taste of the strawberries and lemon.

Nutritional Information (Per Serving): Calories: 160 | Fat: 1g | Carbohydrates: 25g | Protein: 15g

Pineapple Jalapeno Protein Surprise

A sweet and tangy Italian ice with a surprising kick of heat, enhanced with protein for a unique and refreshing treat.

INGREDIENTS

- 1 cup fresh pineapple, chopped
- 1 small jalapeño, seeded and finely chopped
- 1/2 cup coconut water
- 1 scoop vanilla protein powder
- 1 tablespoon lime juice

Prep Time: 5 minutes Skill Level: Easy

Freezing Time: 24 hours Servings: 2

INSTRUCTIONS

1. Blend: In a blender, combine pineapple, jalapeño, coconut water, vanilla protein powder, and lime juice. Blend until smooth.
2. Freeze: Transfer the blended mixture into a Ninja Creami pint container. Freeze for at least 24 hours to ensure it solidifies properly.
3. Italian Ice Function: Place the frozen pint in your Ninja Creami Deluxe and select the "Italian Ice" function. Process until the texture becomes smooth.
4. Re-spin (Optional): For an even smoother texture, select the "Italian Ice" function again to reprocess.
5. Serve: Once the Italian ice reaches the desired consistency, scoop into bowls and enjoy this exotic and spicy treat.

HEALTH BENEFITS

- Vitamin C Boost: Pineapple is high in Vitamin C, supporting immune function and skin health.
- Hydration: Coconut water provides essential electrolytes, making this a great post-workout refreshment.

Nutritional Information (Per Serving): Calories: 180 | Fat: 1g | Carbohydrates: 25g | Protein: 15g

NOTE_____

_____

_____

_____

_____

_____

_____

_____

_____

_____

_____

Spiced Apple Protein Cider

Cozy up with the Spiced Apple Protein Cider, a delightful concoction that brings the classic flavors of autumn to your cup. This Italian ice is infused with apple cider spices and boosted with protein, perfect for enjoying the crisp fall days.

INGREDIENTS

- 1 cup apple cider
- 1/2 teaspoon cinnamon
- A pinch of nutmeg
- 1 scoop vanilla protein powder
- 1 tablespoon maple syrup

Prep Time: 5 minutes Skill Level: Easy

Freezing Time: 24 hours Servings: 2

INSTRUCTIONS

- Blend: Mix apple cider, cinnamon, nutmeg, vanilla protein powder, and maple syrup in a blender until well combined.
- Freeze: Transfer to a Ninja Creami pint container and freeze for 24 hours.
- Italian Ice Function: Use the "Italian Ice" function on your Ninja Creami to create a smooth, flavorful cider ice.
- Re-spin (Optional): If desired, re-spin for a creamier texture.
- Serve: Enjoy this spiced delight as a unique dessert or a refreshing treat.

HEALTH BENEFITS

- Antioxidant Properties: Apples and spices offer antioxidants that can help reduce inflammation and boost health.
- Energy Boost: Ideal for a quick energy lift with natural sugars and protein.

HEALTHY TIPS

Protein Power-Up: Take your spiced apple cider to the next level by blending in a scoop of vanilla protein powder. This will transform your comforting drink into a satisfying, muscle-building treat.

Nutritional Information (Per Serving): Calories: 160 | Fat: 0.5g | Carbohydrates: 28g | Protein: 10g

NOTE_____

_____

_____

_____

_____

_____

_____

_____

_____

Root Beer Protein Float

A nostalgic classic reimagined as a healthier, protein-packed treat, perfect for satisfying your sweet tooth while fueling your muscles.

INGREDIENTS

- 1 cup root beer (diet or regular)
- 1/2 cup milk of choice
- 1 scoop vanilla protein powder
- 1/4 cup mini marshmallows (optional, for mix-ins)

Prep Time: 5 minutes Skill Level: Easy

Freezing Time: 24 hours Servings: 2

INSTRUCTIONS

- Mix: Combine root beer, milk, and protein powder in a Ninja Creami pint. Stir until the protein powder is fully incorporated.
- Freeze: Secure the lid and freeze for at least 24 hours, or until completely solid.
- Process: Place the frozen pint into the Ninja Creami Deluxe and select the "Italian Ice" function.
- Mix-in (Optional): Once the cycle is complete, use a spoon to create a small hole in the center of the ice about 1 1/2 inches deep. Add the mini marshmallows to the hole and use the "Mix-in" program to incorporate them evenly.
- Re-spin (Optional): For a smoother, creamier texture, re-spin once or twice.

HEALTH BENEFITS

- Lower in calories and sugar than traditional root beer floats (especially if using diet root beer).
- Provides a good source of protein for muscle maintenance and recovery.

HEALTHY TIPS

- Opt for diet root beer for a sugar-free version.
- Choose a high-quality protein powder with minimal added sugar or artificial ingredients.

Nutritional Information (Per Serving): Calories: 120 | Fat: 2g | Carbs: 15g | Protein: 10g

NOTE_____

_____

_____

_____

_____

_____

_____

_____

_____

Horchata Protein Spice

A creamy and comforting Italian ice inspired by the traditional Mexican drink, infused with warm spices and protein for a unique and satisfying treat.

INGREDIENTS

- 1 cup rice milk
- 1/2 cup water
- 1 scoop vanilla protein powder
- 1/2 teaspoon cinnamon
- 1/4 teaspoon nutmeg
- Pinch of cloves
- 1/4 cup chopped almonds or walnuts (optional, for mix-ins)

Prep Time: 5 minutes Skill Level: Easy

Freezing Time: 24 hours Servings: 2

INSTRUCTIONS

1. Mix: Combine all ingredients (except for optional mix-ins) in a Ninja Creami pint and stir until the protein powder is fully dissolved.
2. Freeze: Secure the lid and freeze for at least 24 hours, or until completely solid.
3. Process: Place the frozen pint into the Ninja Creami Deluxe and select the "Italian Ice" function.
4. Mix-ins (Optional): Once the cycle is complete, use a spoon to create a small hole in the center of the ice about 1 1/2 inches deep. Add the chopped nuts and use the "Mix-in" program to incorporate them evenly.
5. Re-spin (Optional): For a smoother consistency, re-spin once or twice.

HEALTH BENEFITS

- Naturally dairy-free and can be made vegan-friendly.
- Provides a good source of protein and calcium.

HEALTHY TIPS

- Use unsweetened rice milk to reduce sugar content.
- Add a pinch of cardamom for extra depth of flavor.

Nutritional Information (Per Serving): Calories: 180 | Fat: 3g | Carbs: 22g | Protein: 12g

NOTE_____

_____

_____

_____

_____

_____

_____

_____

_____

Coconut Cream Protein Pie

A rich and decadent treat inspired by the classic dessert, but with added protein for a more filling and nutritious snack.

INGREDIENTS

- 1 cup coconut milk
- 1/2 cup water
- 1 scoop vanilla protein powder
- 1/4 teaspoon coconut extract
- 1/4 cup crushed graham crackers (optional, for mix-ins)
- Sweetener to taste (optional)

Prep Time: 5 minutes Skill Level: Easy

Freezing Time: 24 hours Servings: 2

INSTRUCTIONS

1. Blend: Combine coconut milk, water, protein powder, and coconut extract in a blender. Blend until smooth. Taste and add sweetener if desired.
2. Freeze: Transfer the mixture into a Ninja Creami pint and freeze for at least 24 hours, or until completely solid.
3. Process: Place the frozen pint into the outer bowl of the Ninja Creami Deluxe. Select the "Italian Ice" function and process until is creamy.
4. Mix-in (Optional): Once the cycle is complete, use a spoon to create a small hole in the center of the ice about 1 1/2 inches deep. Add the crushed graham crackers and use the "Mix-in" program to incorporate them evenly.
5. Re-Spin (Optional): For a smoother consistency, re-spin once or twice.

HEALTH BENEFITS

- Coconut milk is a very good source of healthy fats.
- Protein powder provides a boost for muscle repair and recovery.

HEALTHY TIPS

- Choose unsweetened coconut milk for a lower-calorie option.
- If adding graham crackers, opt for whole-grain or low-sugar varieties.

Nutritional Information (Per Serving): Calories: 180 | Fat: 10g | Carbs: 15g | Protein: 12g

NOTE_____

_____

_____

_____

_____

_____

_____

_____

_____

Mixed Berry Protein Refresher

A revitalizing and thirst-quenching Italian ice, blending the sweetness of mixed berries with the creamy texture of protein powder for a healthy and invigorating treat.

INGREDIENTS

- 1 cup frozen mixed berries
- 1 scoop unflavored protein powder
- 1 cup water
- 1/4 cup fresh mint leaves (optional, for mix-ins)
- Sweetener to taste (optional)

Prep Time: 5 minutes Skill Level: Easy

Freezing Time: 24 hours Servings: 2

INSTRUCTIONS

1. Blend: Combine all ingredients (except for the optional mint leaves) in a blender and blend until smooth.
2. Freeze: Transfer the mixture into a Ninja Creami pint and freeze for at least 24 hours, or until completely solid.
3. Process: Place the frozen pint into the Ninja Creami Deluxe and select the "Italian Ice" function.
4. Mix-in (Optional): Once the cycle is complete, use a spoon to create a small hole in the center of the Italian ice about 1 1/2 inches deep. Add chopped fresh mint (if using). Use the "Mix-in" program to incorporate them evenly.
5. Re-Spin (Optional): For a smoother consistency, re-spin once or twice.

HEALTH BENEFITS

- A natural source of antioxidants from mixed berries.
- Provides a boost of protein for muscle recovery.
- Hydrating and refreshing.

HEALTHY TIPS

- For a lower sugar option, choose unsweetened protein powder and omit additional sweetener.
- Add a squeeze of fresh lime or lemon juice for an extra zing.

Nutritional Information (Per Serving):
Calories: 150 | Fat: 2g | Carbs: 20g | Protein: 15g

NOTE_____

_____

_____

_____

_____

_____

_____

_____

_____

Coconut Cardamom Protein Bliss

A creamy and exotic Italian ice, infused with the warm, aromatic flavors of cardamom and the tropical essence of coconut, all while delivering a satisfying dose of protein.

INGREDIENTS

- 1 cup unsweetened coconut milk
- 1/2 cup water
- 1 scoop vanilla protein powder
- 1/4 teaspoon ground cardamom
- Sweetener to taste (optional)
- Chopped toasted almonds or shredded coconut (optional, for mix-ins)

Prep Time: 5 minutes Skill Level: Easy

Freezing Time: 24 hours Servings: 2

INSTRUCTIONS

- Blend: Combine all ingredients (except for optional mix-ins) in a blender and blend until smooth.
- Freeze: Transfer the mixture into a Ninja Creami pint and freeze for at least 24 hours.
- Process: Place the frozen pint into the Ninja Creami Deluxe and select the "Italian Ice" function.
- Mix-In (Optional): Once the cycle is complete, use a spoon to create a small hole in the center of the Italian ice about 1 1/2 inches deep. Add the chopped almonds or shredded coconut. Use the "Mix-in" program to incorporate them evenly.
- Re-spin (Optional): For a smoother consistency, re-spin once or twice.

HEALTH BENEFITS

- Provides a good source of protein and healthy fats.
- Cardamom is known to have digestive and anti-inflammatory properties.

HEALTHY TIPS

- Add a pinch of cinnamon for an extra layer of warmth and spice.

Nutritional Information (Per Serving): Calories: 150 | Fat: 8g | Carbs: 10g | Protein: 12g

NOTE_____

_____

_____

_____

_____

_____

_____

_____

_____

Chocolate Banana Protein

A decadent and satisfying Italian ice that tastes like a frosty chocolate-covered banana, packed with protein to fuel your day.

INGREDIENTS

- 1 ripe banana
- 1 scoop chocolate protein powder
- 1 cup milk of choice
- 1/4 cup unsweetened cocoa powder
- Sweetener to taste (optional)
- Mini chocolate chips (optional, for mix-ins)

Prep Time: 5 minutes Skill Level: Easy

Freezing Time: 24 hours Servings: 2

INSTRUCTIONS

1. Blend: Combine all ingredients (except for optional mix-ins) in a blender and blend until smooth.
2. Freeze: Transfer the mixture into a Ninja Creami pint and freeze for at least 24 hours.
3. Process: Place the frozen pint into the Ninja Creami Deluxe and select the "Italian Ice" function.
4. Mix-In (Optional): Once the cycle is complete, use a spoon to create a small hole in the center of the Italian ice about 1 1/2 inches deep. Add the mini chocolate chips. Use the "Mix-in" program to incorporate them evenly.
5. Re-spin (Optional): For a smoother consistency, re-spin once or twice.

HEALTH BENEFITS

- Provides a good source of protein for muscle repair and recovery.
- Bananas are a very good source of potassium and fiber.
- Chocolate is a mood booster and contains antioxidants.

HEALTHY TIPS

- Use unsweetened protein powder and milk to control the sugar content.
- To obtain a richer chocolate flavor, use dark cocoa powder.

Nutritional Information (Per Serving): Calories: 180 Fat: 4g Carbs: 25gProtein: 15g

"Unleash your culinary ninja skills and transform your physique.

Every bite brings you closer to your health and fitness goals."

Fruity Fiesta Protein Shake

A burst of fruity flavors and protein, this vibrant milkshake is a refreshing and nutritious way to cool down and recharge.

INGREDIENTS

- 1 cup fruit-flavored protein shake (choose your favorite flavor, like strawberry, mango, or mixed berry)
- 1/2 cup milk of choice
- 1/2 cup frozen fruit chunks

Prep Time: 5 minutes Skill Level: Easy

Freezing Time: 24 hours Servings: 2

INSTRUCTION

1. Blend: Combine the protein shake, milk, and frozen fruit in a blender. Blend until smooth.
2. Freeze: Transfer the mixture into a Ninja Creami pint, ensuring not to overfill. Freeze for at least 24 hours.
3. Process: Place the frozen pint in your Ninja Creami Deluxe and select the "Milkshake" function.
4. Re-spin (Optional): For a smoother consistency, re-spin once or twice.
5. Enjoy Sip on your vibrant and flavorful fruity fiesta protein shake!

HEALTH BENEFITS

- It provides a very good source of protein for muscle recovery.
- It is packed with vitamins and antioxidants from the fruit.
- Hydrating and refreshing.

HEALTHY TIPS

- Choose a low-sugar or unsweetened fruit-flavored protein shake.
- Add a handful of spinach or kale for a boost of greens.
- Use seasonal fruits for the freshest flavor and maximum nutritional value.

Nutritional Information (Per Serving): Calories: 220 | Fat: 5g | Carbs: 30g | Protein: 20g

Minty Chocolate Chip Protein Shake

A refreshing and decadent milkshake that combines the cool taste of mint with rich chocolate, all while packing a protein punch for a healthy twist on a classic treat.

INGREDIENTS

- 1 cup mint chocolate chip protein shake
- 1/2 cup milk of choice

- 1/4 cup mini chocolate chips (for mix-ins)

Prep Time: 5 minutes Skill Level: Easy

Freezing Time: 24 hours Servings: 2

INSTRUCTION

1. Blend: Combine the protein shake and milk in a blender. Blend until smooth.
2. Freeze: Transfer the mixture into a Ninja Creami pint, ensuring not to overfill. Freeze for at least 24 hours.
3. Process: Place the frozen pint in your Ninja Creami Deluxe and select the "Milkshake" function.
4. Mix-In: Create a small hole in the center of the milkshake about 1 1/2 inches deep using a spoon. Add the mini chocolate chips and use the "Mix-in" program to incorporate them evenly.
5. Re-spin (Optional): For a smoother consistency, re-spin once or twice.
6. Enjoy Sip on your cool and creamy minty chocolate chip protein shake!

HEALTH BENEFITS

- Protein shake provides a substantial amount of protein for muscle growth and repair.
- Contains calcium from milk for strong bones.

- Mint can aid digestion and freshen breath.

HEALTHY TIPS

- Use a low-sugar or unsweetened mint chocolate chip protein shake.
- Add a handful of spinach or kale for a hidden dose of greens.
- If you like your milkshake extra minty, add a few drops of mint extract.

Nutritional Information (Per Serving): Calories: 200 | Fat: 5g | Carbs: 25g | Protein: 20g

Coffee Lover's Protein Pick-Me-Up

A creamy and energizing coffee milkshake, infused with protein for sustained energy and a delicious kick.

INGREDIENTS

- 1 cup coffee protein shake
- 1/2 cup milk of choice
- 1 shot espresso (optional)

Prep Time: 5 minutes Skill Level: Easy

Freezing Time: 24 hours Servings: 2

INSTRUCTIONS

1. Blend: Combine the coffee protein shake, milk, and espresso shot (if using) in a blender. Blend until smooth.

2. Freeze: Transfer the mixture into a Ninja Creami pint, ensuring not to overfill. Freeze for at least 24 hours.

3. Process: Place the frozen pint in your Ninja Creami Deluxe and select the "Milkshake" function.

4. Re-spin (Optional): For a smoother consistency, re-spin once or twice.

5. Enjoy Sip on your protein-packed coffee pick-me-up!

HEALTH BENEFITS

- Coffee provides antioxidants and a natural energy boost.
- Protein shake promotes muscle recovery and satiety.

HEALTHY TIPS

- Use a low-sugar or unsweetened coffee protein shake for a healthier option.
- Opt for a sugar-free or low-fat whipped cream topping.

Nutritional Information (Per Serving): Calories: 180 | Fat: 5g | Carbs: 15g | Protein: 20g

Oatmeal Cookie Protein Shake

Luxuriate in the comforting taste of oatmeal cookies in a protein-rich milkshake that is both delicious and satisfying.

INGREDIENTS

- 1 cup oatmeal cookie-flavored protein shake
- 1/2 cup milk of choice
- 1/4 cup crushed oats
- 1/4 teaspoon cinnamon
- 1/4 cup of chocolate syrup

Prep Time: 5 minutes Skill Level: Easy

Freezing Time: 24 hours Servings: 2

INSTRUCTIONS

1. Blend: Combine the protein shake, milk, crushed oats, and cinnamon in a blender. Blend until smooth.

2. Freeze: Transfer the mixture into a Ninja Creami pint, ensuring not to overfill. Freeze for at least 24 hours.

3. Process: Place the frozen pint in your Ninja Creami Deluxe and select the "Milkshake" function.

4. Mix-in (Optional): Create a small hole in the center of the milkshake about 1 1/2 inches deep using a spoon. Add chocolate syrup and use the "Mix-in" program to incorporate them evenly.

5. Enjoy Sip on your comforting and nutritious oatmeal cookie protein shake!

HEALTH BENEFITS

- Protein shake provides a good source of protein for muscle growth and repair.
- Oats are a good source of fiber, which aids in digestion.
- Cinnamon may help regulate blood sugar levels.

HEALTHY TIPS

- Choose a low-sugar or unsweetened oatmeal cookie protein shake.
- Use rolled oats or quick oats for a fiber boost.
- Add a handful of chopped nuts for extra protein and healthy fats.

Nutritional Information (Per Serving): Calories: 280 | Fat: 10g | Carbs: 35g | Protein: 22g

Double Chocolate Malt

A rich and decadent milkshake featuring double the chocolate flavor with a hint of malt for a classic treat.

INGREDIENTS

- 1 cup chocolate protein shake
- 1/2 cup milk of choice
- 2 tablespoons chocolate malt powder
- 1/4 cup mini chocolate chips (for mix-ins)

Prep Time: 5 minutes Skill Level: Easy

Freezing Time: 24 hours Servings: 2

INSTRUCTIONS

1. Blend: Combine the protein shake, milk, and chocolate malt powder in a blender. Blend until smooth.
2. Freeze: Transfer the mixture into a Ninja Creami pint, ensuring not to overfill. Freeze for at least 24 hours.
3. Process: Place the frozen pint in your Ninja Creami Deluxe and select the "Milkshake" function.
4. Mix-In: Create a small hole in the center of the milkshake about 1 1/2 inches deep using a spoon. Add the mini chocolate chips and use the "Mix-in" program to incorporate them evenly.
5. Enjoy Sip on your decadent double chocolate malt protein shake!

HEALTH BENEFITS

- Protein shake provides a good source of protein for muscle growth and repair.
- Malt powder contains B vitamins and minerals.

HEALTHY TIPS

- Use a low-sugar or unsweetened chocolate protein shake.
- Opt for a high-quality chocolate malt powder with minimal added sugar.

Nutritional Information (Per Serving):
Calories: 250 | Fat: 8g | Carbs: 28g | Protein: 20g

Cookies & Cream Protein Overload

A decadent cookies and cream milkshake loaded with protein for a guilt-free indulgence.

INGREDIENTS:

- 1 cup cookies and cream protein shake
- 1/2 cup milk of choice
- **4-5 crushed Oreo cookies (for mix-ins)**

Prep Time: 5 minutes Skill Level: Easy

Freezing Time: 24 hours Servings: 2

INSTRUCTIONS

1. Blend: Combine the protein shake and milk in a blender. Blend the mixture until smooth.
2. Freeze: Transfer the mixture into a Ninja Creami pint, ensuring not to overfill. Freeze for at least 24 hours.
3. Process: Place the frozen pint in your Ninja Creami Deluxe and select the "Milkshake" function.
4. Mix-In: Create a small hole in the center of the milkshake about 1 1/2 inches deep using a spoon. Add the crushed Oreo cookies and use the "Mix-in" program to incorporate them evenly.
5. Enjoy Sip on your rich and creamy cookies and cream protein milkshake!

HEALTH BENEFITS

- Protein shake provides a substantial amount of protein for muscle growth and repair.
- Contains calcium from milk for strong bones.

HEALTHY TIPS

- Use a low-sugar or unsweetened cookies and cream protein shake.
- You can substitute the Oreo cookies with other healthy cookie options like protein cookies or homemade oatmeal cookies.

Nutritional Information (Per Serving):
Calories: 250 | Fat: 8g | Carbs: 28g | Protein: 22g

Almond Joy Protein Shake

A decadent milkshake that captures the iconic Almond Joy flavors of chocolate, almond, and coconut in a protein-rich treat.

INGREDIENTS

- 1 cup chocolate protein shake
- 1/2 cup unsweetened almond milk
- 1/4 cup shredded coconut (unsweetened)
- 1 tablespoon almond butter
- 1/4 teaspoon almond extract (optional)
- 1/4 cup chopped almonds or mini chocolate chips (optional, for mix-ins)

Prep Time: 5 minutes Skill Level: Easy

Freezing Time: 24 hours Servings: 2

INSTRUCTIONS

1. Blend: Combine all ingredients (except for optional mix-ins) in a blender and blend until smooth and creamy.
2. Freeze: Transfer the mixture into a Ninja Creami pint, ensuring not to overfill. Freeze for at least 24 hours.
3. Process: Place the frozen pint in your Ninja Creami Deluxe and select the "Milkshake" function.
4. Mix-In (Optional): Create a small hole in the center of the milkshake about 1 1/2 inches deep using a spoon. Add the chopped almonds or mini chocolate chips and use the "Mix-in" program to incorporate them evenly.
5. Enjoy Sip on your luxurious Almond Joy Protein Shake!

HEALTH BENEFITS

- Provides a good source of protein for muscle growth and repair.
- Almond butter offers healthy fats and additional protein.
- Coconut provides electrolytes, which may boost energy.

HEALTHY TIPS

- Use unsweetened almond milk and shredded coconut to reduce sugar intake.
- Choose a high-quality chocolate protein powder with minimal added sugar.

Nutritional Information (Per Serving): Calories: 280 | Fat: 15g | Carbs: 20g | Protein: 22g

NOTE_____

_____

_____

_____

_____

_____

_____

_____

Raspberry Cheesecake Protein Shake

A creamy and tangy milkshake that captures the essence of raspberry cheesecake, packed with protein for a guilt-free indulgence.

INGREDIENTS

- 1 cup vanilla protein shake
- 1/2 cup milk of choice
- 1/2 cup frozen raspberries
- 1/4 cup crumbled graham crackers (for mix-ins)

Prep Time: 5 minutes Skill Level: Easy

Freezing Time: 24 hours Servings: 2

INSTRUCTIONS

1. Blend: Combine protein shake, milk, and frozen raspberries in a blender. Blend until smooth and creamy.
2. Freeze: Transfer the mixture into a Ninja Creami pint, ensuring not to overfill. Freeze for at least 24 hours.
3. Process: Place the frozen pint in your Ninja Creami Deluxe and select the "Milkshake" function.
4. Mix-In: Create a small hole in the center of the milkshake about 1 1/2 inches deep using a spoon. Add the crumbled graham crackers and use the "Mix-in" program to incorporate them evenly.
5. Enjoy Sip on your delightful Raspberry Cheesecake Protein Shake!

HEALTH BENEFITS

- Raspberries provide antioxidants and fiber.
- Protein shake promotes muscle recovery and satiety.

HEALTHY TIPS

- Use a low-sugar or unsweetened vanilla protein shake for a healthier option.
- Add a tablespoon of cream cheese for extra richness

Nutritional Information (Per Serving): Calories: 220 | Fat: 5g | Carbs: 28g | Protein: 20g

NOTE_____

_____

_____

_____

_____

_____

_____

_____

_____

_____

_____

Mango Pineapple Protein Shake

A refreshing tropical milkshake that combines the sweetness of mango and the tang of pineapple with a boost of protein.

INGREDIENTS

- 1 cup vanilla protein shake
- 1/2 cup frozen mango chunks
- 1/2 cup frozen pineapple chunks
- 1/4 cup orange juice
- Toasted coconut flakes (optional, for mix-ins)

Prep Time: 5 minutes Skill Level: Easy

Freezing Time: 24 hours Servings: 2

INSTRUCCTIONS

1. Blend: Combine all ingredients (except optional mix-ins) in a blender and blend until smooth.
2. Freeze: Transfer the mixture into a Ninja Creami pint, ensuring not to overfill. Freeze for at least 24 hours.
3. Process: Place the frozen pint in your Ninja Creami Deluxe and select the "Milkshake" function.
4. Mix-In (Optional): Create a small hole in the center of the milkshake about 1 1/2 inches deep using a spoon. Add the toasted coconut flakes and use the "Mix-in" program to incorporate them evenly.
5. Enjoy Sip on your tropical Mango Pineapple Protein Shake!

HEALTH BENEFITS

- It is a very good source of vitamins A and C.
- Supports digestion and hydration with the combination of fruits and protein.

HEALTHY TIPS

- Use more of fresh or frozen fruit for the best flavor.
- You can Add a squeeze of lime juice for extra zing.

Nutritional Information (Per Serving):
Calories: 200 | Fat: 3g | Carbs: 30g | Protein: 18g

NOTE_____

_____

_____

_____

_____

_____

_____

_____

_____

_____

_____

Build-Your-Own Protein Shake

A customizable protein milkshake experience, allowing you to create your perfect combination of flavors and nutrients.

INGREDIENTS

- 1 cup protein shake base (choose your favorite flavor)
- 1/2 cup milk of choice
- Mix-in options:
- Fruits: berries, banana, mango
- Seeds: chia seeds, flaxseeds, hemp seeds
- Other: cocoa powder, vanilla extract, maple syrup

Prep Time: 5 minutes Skill Level: Easy

Freezing Time: 24 hours Servings: 2

INSTRUCTIONS

1. Blend: Combine the protein shake base and milk in a blender. Add your chosen mix-ins and blend until smooth and creamy.
2. Freeze: Transfer the mixture into a Ninja Creami pint, ensuring not to overfill. Freeze for at least 24 hours.
3. Process: Place the frozen pint in your Ninja Creami Deluxe and select the "Milkshake" function.
4. Mix-In (Optional): Create a small hole in the center of the milkshake about 1 1/2 inches deep using a spoon. Add the toasted coconut flakes and use the "Mix-in" program to incorporate them evenly.
5. Enjoy Sip on your personalized protein shake creation!

HEALTH BENEFITS

- Customizable to fit your dietary needs and preferences.
- It provides a good source of protein for muscle recovery and satiety.
- Can be tailored to include a variety of vitamins, minerals, and antioxidants.

HEALTHY TIPS

- Choose a low-sugar or unsweetened protein shake base.
- Opt for natural mix-ins like fruits, nuts, and seeds.
- Limit the use of sugary or processed mix-ins

"Embrace the power of protein and unlock your full potential.

Nourish your body and mind with every creamy creation."

Blueberry Muffin Protein

A delicious blend of coffee and blueberry muffin flavors, packed with protein to fuel your day.

INGREDIENTS

- 1 cup cold brew coffee
- 1/2 cup frozen blueberries
- 1/2 scoop vanilla protein powder
- 1/4 cup milk of choice
- 1/4 cup oats
- 1/2 tsp cinnamon
- Sweetener to taste (optional)
- Crumbled blueberry muffin or granola (optional, for mix-ins)

Prep Time: 5 minutes Skill Level: Easy

Freezing Time: 24 hours Servings: 1

INSTRUCTIONS

1. Blend: Combine all ingredients (except for optional mix-ins) in the Ninja Creami blender and blend until smooth.
2. Freeze: Pour the mixture into a Ninja Creami pint and freeze for at least 24 hours, or until completely solid.
3. Process: Place the frozen pint in your Ninja Creami Deluxe and select the "Creamiccino" function.
4. Re-spin (Optional): Re-spin once or twice for a creamier consistency.
5. Mix-In (Optional): Create a small hole in the center of the frozen treat about 1 1/2 inches deep using a spoon. Add crumbled blueberry muffin or granola and use the "Mix-in" program to incorporate them evenly.

HEALTH BENEFITS

- Blueberries are packed with antioxidants, which may protect against cell damage.
- Oats are a good source of fiber, which helps promote healthy digestion.
- Protein powder supports muscle repair and provides sustained energy.

HEALTHY TIPS

- Use unsweetened almond milk for a lower calorie option.
- Use a natural sweetener such as honey or maple syrup.
- Choose a high-quality protein powder with minimal added sugar.

Nutritional Information (Per Serving):
Calories: 250 | Fat: 7g | Carbs: 30g | Protein: 18g

Citrus Buzz Protein Creamiccino

A zesty and energizing coffee drink with a bright citrus twist and a protein boost to kick-start your day.

INGREDIENTS

- 1 cup cold brew coffee
- 1/4 cup orange juice
- 1/4 cup grapefruit juice
- 1/2 scoop vanilla protein powder
- Sweetener to taste (optional)
- Orange zest (optional, for mix-ins)

Prep Time: 5 minutes Skill Level: Easy

Freezing Time: 24 hours Servings: 1

INSTRUCTIONS

1. Blend: Combine all ingredients (except for optional mix-ins) in the Ninja Creami blender and blend until smooth.
2. Freeze: Pour the mixture into a Ninja Creami pint and freeze for at least 24 hours, or until completely solid.
3. Process: Place the frozen pint in your Ninja Creami Deluxe and select the "Creamiccino" function.
4. Re-spin (Optional): Re-spin once or twice for a creamier consistency.
5. Mix-In (Optional): Create a small hole in the center of the frozen treat about 1 1/2 inches deep using a spoon. Add orange zest and use the "Mix-in" program to incorporate them evenly.

HEALTH BENEFITS

- Citrus fruits are a great source of Vitamin C for immune support.
- Protein powder provides a boost of energy and helps with muscle recovery.

HEALTHY TIPS

- Use freshly squeezed orange and grapefruit juice for the most vibrant flavor.
- If you prefer a sweeter drink, add a natural sweetener like honey or agave.

Nutritional Information (Per Serving):
Calories: 150 | Fat: 2g | Carbs: 18g | Protein: 15g

NOTE_____

_____

_____

_____

_____

_____

_____

_____

_____

_____

Raspberry Cocoa Protein Creamiccino

A decadent and fruity coffee treat, blending the tartness of raspberries with rich cocoa and a protein boost for a satisfying indulgence.

INGREDIENTS

- 1 cup cold brew coffee
- 1/2 cup frozen raspberries
- 1/2 scoop chocolate protein powder
- 1/4 cup milk of choice
- 1 tablespoon unsweetened cocoa powder
- Sweetener to taste (optional)

Prep Time: 5 minutes Skill Level: Easy

Freezing Time: 24 hours Servings: 1

INSTRUCTIONS

1. Blend: Combine all ingredients in the Ninja Creami blender and blend until smooth.
2. Freeze: Pour the mixture into a Ninja Creami pint and freeze for at least 24 hours.
3. Process: Place the frozen pint in your Ninja Creami Deluxe and select the "Creamiccino" function.
4. Re-Spin (Optional): Re-spin once or twice for a creamier consistency.

HEALTH BENEFITS

- Raspberries are packed with antioxidants and fiber, promoting a healthy gut and immune system.
- Cocoa powder provides a boost of antioxidants and minerals.
- Protein powder supports muscle recovery and satiety.

HEALTHY TIPS

- Use unsweetened almond milk for a lower-calorie option.
- Use a natural sweetener such as honey or maple syrup.
- Add a handful of spinach or kale for a hidden dose of greens.

Nutritional Information (Per Serving):
Calories: 200 | Fat: 5g | Carbs: 25g | Protein: 18g

NOTE_____

_____

_____

_____

_____

_____

_____

_____

_____

_____

_____

Caramel Apple Protein Creamiccino

A delightful fall-inspired coffee treat with warm spices, sweet caramel, and a protein boost to keep you going.

INGREDIENTS

- 1 cup cold brew coffee
- 1/2 cup chopped apple (peeled)
- 1/2 scoop vanilla protein powder
- 1/4 cup milk of choice
- 1/4 teaspoon cinnamon
- 1 tablespoon caramel sauce (optional, for mix-ins)

Prep Time: 5 minutes Skill Level: Easy

Freezing Time: 24 hours Servings: 1

INSTRUCTIONS

1. Blend: Combine all ingredients (except the optional caramel sauce) in the Ninja Creami blender and blend until smooth.
2. Freeze: Pour the mixture into a Ninja Creami pint and freeze for at least 24 hours, or until completely solid.
3. Process: Place the frozen pint in your Ninja Creami Deluxe and select the "Creamiccino" function.
4. Re-spin (Optional): Re-spin once or twice for a creamier consistency.
5. Mix-In (Optional): Create a small hole in the center of the frozen treat about 1 1/2 inches deep using a spoon. Add caramel sauce and use the "Mix-in" program to incorporate it evenly.

HEALTH BENEFITS

- Apples provide fiber and antioxidants.
- Protein powder aids in muscle repair and provides sustained energy.
- Cinnamon may help regulate blood sugar levels.

HEALTHY TIPS

- Use a tart apple variety like Granny Smith for a balanced flavor.
- Choose a sugar-free or low-sugar caramel sauce.
- Add a dash of nutmeg or allspice for additional warmth.

Nutritional Information (Per Serving): Calories: 190 | Fat: 4g | Carbs: 25g | Protein: 15g

NOTE_____

_____

_____

_____

_____

_____

_____

Pumpkin Spice Protein Creamiccino

A warm and inviting coffee drink reminiscent of fall, combining the comforting flavors of pumpkin spice with a protein boost for a satisfying and healthy treat.

INGREDIENTS

- 1 cup cold brew coffee
- 1/4 cup pumpkin puree
- 1/2 scoop vanilla protein powder
- 1/4 cup milk of choice
- 1/2 teaspoon pumpkin pie spice
- Sweetener to taste (optional)
- Whipped cream and a sprinkle of pumpkin pie spice (optional, for mix-ins)

Prep Time: 5 minute Skill Level: Easy

Freezing Time: 24 hours Servings: 1

INSTRUCTION

1. Blend: Combine cold brew coffee, pumpkin puree, protein powder, milk, pumpkin pie spice, and sweetener (if using) in a blender. Blend until smooth.
2. Freeze: Pour the mixture into a Ninja Creami pint and freeze for at least 24 hours, or until completely solid.
3. Process: Place the frozen pint in your Ninja Creami Deluxe and select the "Creamiccino" function.
4. Re-Spin (Optional): Re-spin once or twice for a creamier consistency.
5. Mix-In (Optional): Create a small hole in the center of the frozen treat about 1 1/2 inches deep using a spoon. Add whipped cream and sprinkle with pumpkin pie spice, and then use the "Mix-in" program to incorporate them evenly.

HEALTH BENEFITS

- Pumpkin puree is a good source of Vitamin A and fiber.
- Protein powder provides a boost of energy and helps with muscle recovery.
- Spices like cinnamon and nutmeg may have anti-inflammatory properties.

HEALTHY TIPS:

- Use unsweetened almond milk for a lower-calorie option.
- Choose a high-quality protein powder with minimal added sugar.

Nutritional Information (Per Serving):
Calories: 220 | Fat: 5g | Carbs: 25g | Protein: 18g

Maple Cinnamon Latte Protein Creamiccino

A comforting and warm-spiced coffee drink with a touch of sweetness and a boost of protein for a delightful morning pick-me-up.

INGREDIENTS

- 1 cup cold brew coffee
- 1/2 scoop vanilla protein powder
- 1/4 cup milk of choice
- 1 tablespoon maple syrup
- 1/2 teaspoon cinnamon
- Whipped cream and a sprinkle of cinnamon (optional, for mix-ins)

Prep Time: 5 minutes Skill Level: Easy

Freezing Time: 24 hours Servings: 1

INSTRUCTIONS

1. Blend: Combine all ingredients (except for optional mix-ins) in the Ninja Creami blender and blend until smooth.
2. Freeze: Pour the mixture into a Ninja Creami pint and freeze for at least 24 hours, or until completely solid.
3. Process: Place the frozen pint in your Ninja Creami Deluxe and select the "Creamiccino" function.
4. Re-Spin (Optional): Re-spin once or twice for a creamier consistency.
5. Mix-In (Optional): Create a small hole in the center of the frozen treat about 1 1/2 inches deep using a spoon. Add whipped cream and sprinkle with cinnamon, and then use the "Mix-in" program to incorporate them evenly.

HEALTH BENEFITS

- Maple syrup is a natural sweetener with some antioxidants.
- Cinnamon may help regulate blood sugar levels.
- Protein powder supports muscle recovery and satiety.

HEALTHY TIPS

- Use unsweetened almond milk for a lower-calorie option.
- Adjust the amount of maple syrup to your preferred sweetness level.
- Add a pinch of nutmeg or allspice for additional warmth.

Nutritional Information (Per Serving):
Calories: 200 | Fat: 5g | Carbs: 20g | Protein: 18g

"Awaken your inner warrior with every protein-packed recipe."

Sunrise Protein Smoothie

A vibrant and refreshing frozen drink that tastes like a tropical sunrise, packed with protein to fuel your day.

INGREDIENTS

- 1 cup frozen mango chunks
- 1/2 cup frozen pineapple chunks
- 1/2 cup orange juice
- 1/2 scoop vanilla protein powder
- 1/4 cup milk of choice (optional, for extra creaminess)
- Shredded coconut, granola, or chopped nuts (optional, for mix-in)

Prep Time: 5 minutes Skill Level: Easy

Freezing Time: 24 hours Servings: 1

INSTRUCTIONS

1. Blend: Combine all ingredients (except for optional mix-ins) in the Ninja Creami blender and blend until smooth and creamy. If desired, add a few ice cubes for an extra-chilled drink.
2. Freeze: Pour the mixture into a Ninja Creami pint and freeze for 24 hours, or until completely solid.
3. Process: Place the frozen pint into the Ninja Creami Deluxe and select the "Frozen Drink" function.
4. Re-Spin (Optional): Re-spin once or twice for a smoother consistency.
5. Mix-In (Optional): Create a small hole in the center of the frozen drink about 1 1/2 inches deep using a spoon. Add your desired mix-ins and use the "Mix-in" program to incorporate them evenly.

HEALTH BENEFITS

- Packed with vitamins and antioxidants from the mango and pineapple.
- Provides a boost of protein for sustained energy and muscle recovery.

HEALTHY TIPS

- Use fresh or frozen fruit for the best flavor and texture.
- If you prefer a thicker smoothie, reduce the amount of liquid or add a few ice cubes.
- Choose a protein powder with minimal added sugar or artificial ingredients.

Nutritional Information (Per Serving):
Calories: 200 | Fat: 5g | Carbs: 30g | Protein: 15g

Frozen Protein Mudslide

A decadent and indulgent frozen cocktail with a protein boost, perfect for a special occasion or a guilt-free treat.

INGREDIENTS

- 1/2 cup cold brew coffee
- 1/4 cup milk of choice
- 1 scoop chocolate protein powder
- 1 ounce coffee liqueur (optional)
- 1 ounce Irish cream liqueur (optional)
- Mini chocolate chips or crushed cookies (optional, for mix-ins)

Prep Time: 5 minutes Skill Level: Easy

Freezing Time: 24 hours Servings: 1

INSTRUCTIONS

1. Blend: Combine all ingredients (except for optional garnishes) in the Ninja Creami blender and blend until smooth.
2. Freeze: Pour the mixture into a Ninja Creami pint and freeze for at least 24 hours, or until completely solid.
3. Process: Place the frozen pint in your Ninja Creami Deluxe and select the "Frozen Drink" function.
4. Re-Spin (Optional): Re-spin once or twice for a smoother consistency.
5. Mix-In (Optional): Create a small hole in the center of the frozen drink about 1 1/2 inches deep using a spoon. Add your mix-ins and use the "Mix-in" program to incorporate them evenly.

HEALTH BENEFITS

- Coffee provides antioxidants and a natural energy boost.
- Protein powder supports muscle recovery and satiety.

HEALTHY TIPS

- Use a low-sugar or unsweetened protein powder.
- Omit or reduce the amount of liqueurs for a lower-calorie option.

Nutritional Information (Per Serving): Calories: 250 | Fat: 10g | Carbs: 15g | Protein: 20g

NOTE_____

_____

_____

_____

_____

_____

_____

_____

_____

_____

Watermelon Protein Frosé

A refreshing and sophisticated frozen cocktail combining the sweetness of watermelon with the subtle notes of rosé wine and a boost of protein.

INGREDIENTS

- 2 cups frozen watermelon chunks
- 1/2 cup rosé wine
- 1/4 cup lime juice
- 1 scoop unflavored protein powder
- Fresh mint leaves or frozen raspberries (optional, for mix-ins)

Prep Time: 5 minutes Skill Level: Easy

Freezing Time: 24 hours Servings: 2

INSTRUCTIONS

1. Blend: Combine all ingredients (except optional mix-ins) in a blender and blend until smooth.
2. Freeze: Pour the mixture into a Ninja Creami pint, ensuring not to overfill. Freeze for at least 24 hours, or until completely solid.
3. Process: Place the frozen pint in your Ninja Creami Deluxe and select the "Frozen Drink" function.
4. Re-Spin (Optional): Re-spin once or twice for a smoother consistency.
5. Mix-In (Optional): Create a small hole in the center of the frozen drink about 1 1/2 inches deep using a spoon. Add your mix-ins and use the "Mix-in" program to incorporate them evenly.

HEALTH BENEFITS

- Watermelon is hydrating and rich in electrolytes.
- Provides a good source of protein for muscle recovery.
- Rosé wine contains antioxidants.

HEALTHY TIPS

- Choose a dry rosé wine for a lower sugar content.
- Use a high-quality unflavored protein powder without artificial sweeteners.

Nutritional Information (Per Serving): Calories: 150 | Fat: 0g | Carbs: 15g | Protein: 12g

NOTE_____

_____

_____

_____

_____

_____

_____

_____

_____

_____

Spiced Pear & Ginger Protein Shake

A warm and comforting milkshake with the sweetness of pear, the subtle spice of ginger, and a boost of protein to keep you satisfied. It is like a hug in a glass, perfect for chilly mornings or a cozy afternoon snack.

INGREDIENTS

- 1 cup unsweetened almond milk
- 1/2 cup frozen pear chunks
- 1/2 scoop vanilla protein powder
- 1/2 inch piece fresh ginger, peeled and grated
- 1/4 teaspoon cinnamon

Prep Time: 5 minutes Skill Level: Easy

Freezing Time: 24 hours Servings: 1

INSTRUCTIONS

1. Blend: Toss everything into your Ninja Creami blender and give it a whirl until it's perfectly smooth and creamy.
2. Freeze: Pour the mixture into a Ninja Creami pint, making sure not to fill it up too much. Pop it in the freezer for at least 24 hours, until it's frozen solid.
3. Process: Now for the fun part! Place the frozen pint in your Ninja Creami Deluxe and select the "Frozen Drink" function. Watch the magic happen!
4. Re-Spin (Optional): If you would like a thicker, more sippable consistency, give it a re-spin or two.

HEALTH BENEFITS

- Pears are a fantastic source of fiber, helping to keep your digestive system happy.
- Ginger adds a bit of zing and is known for its soothing properties for an upset stomach.
- A scoop of protein powder not only gives this smoothie staying power but also helps with muscle recovery and building.

HEALTHY TIPS

- For an extra burst of flavor, use a ripe pear. You can even try swapping the almond milk for a pear-flavored milk alternative for a double dose of pear goodness!

Nutritional Information (Per Serving): Calories: 200 | Fat: 5g | Carbs: 25g | Protein: 15g

Green Machine Protein Shake

A revitalizing and refreshing frozen drink packed with the goodness of leafy greens, tropical fruit, and protein, this vibrant green shake is a healthy and energizing way to start your day or refuel your energy after a workout.

INGREDIENTS

- 1 cup spinach or kale
- 1/2 cup frozen pineapple chunks
- 1/2 banana
- 1 scoop vanilla protein powder
- 1/2 cup water or coconut water
- Chia seeds or hemp seeds (optional, for mix-ins)

Prep Time: 5 minutes Skill Level: Easy

Freezing Time: 24 hours Servings: 1

INSTRUCTIONS

1. Blend: Combine all ingredients (except for optional mix-ins) in your Ninja Creami blender. Blend until smooth and creamy.
2. Freeze: Pour the mixture into a Ninja Creami pint, making sure not to overfill. Freeze for at least 24 h Process: Place the frozen pint in your Ninja Creami Deluxe and select the "Frozen Drink" function.
3. Re-Spin (Optional): Re-spin once or twice for a creamier consistency.
4. Mix-In (Optional): Create a small hole in the center of the frozen drink about 1 1/2 inches deep using a spoon. Add Chia seeds or hemp seeds and use the "Mix-in" program to incorporate them evenly.ours, or until completely solid.

HEALTH BENEFITS

- Green Machine Protein Shakes are packed with vitamins, minerals, and antioxidants from leafy greens and fruits, promoting overall health and well-being.
- Energy and Recovery Fuel: The combination of protein and complex carbohydrates in Green Machine shakes provides sustained energy for workouts and daily activities.

HEALTHY TIPS

- Do not limit yourself to one recipe! Experiment with different leafy greens like spinach, kale, and romaine lettuce, and add a variety of fruits for a unique flavor profile and a wider range of nutrients.

Nutritional Information (Per Serving):
Calories: 150 | Fat: 0g | Carbs: 15g | Protein: 12g

Banana Bread Protein Shake

A comforting, protein-rich frozen drink that tastes just like your favorite banana bread in a glass, perfect for a healthy breakfast or snack.

INGREDIENTS

- 1 cup banana bread protein shake
- 1/2 cup milk of choice
- 1/4 cup frozen banana slices
- 1/4 teaspoon cinnamon
- Crumbled banana bread or granola (optional, for mix-ins)

Prep Time: 5 minutes Skill Level: Easy

Freezing Time: 24 hours Servings: 1

INSTRUCTIONS

1. Blend: Combine all ingredients (except for optional mix-ins) in the Ninja Creami blender and blend until smooth.
2. Freeze: Pour the mixture into a Ninja Creami pint, ensuring not to overfill. Freeze for at least 24 hours, or until completely solid.
3. Process: Place the frozen pint in your Ninja Creami Deluxe and select the "Frozen Drink" function.
4. Re-Spin (Optional): Re-spin once or twice for a creamier consistency.
5. Mix-In (Optional): Create a small hole in the center of the frozen drink about 1 1/2 inches deep using a spoon. Add crumbled banana bread or granola and use the "Mix-in" program to incorporate them evenly.

HEALTH BENEFITS

- Bananas provide potassium and fiber.
- Protein shake promotes muscle recovery and satiety.
- Cinnamon may help regulate blood sugar levels.

HEALTHY TIPS

- Use a ripe banana for extra sweetness.
- Choose a low-sugar or unsweetened vanilla protein shake.

Nutritional Information (Per Serving):
Calories: 250 | Fat: 5g | Carbs: 35g | Protein: 20g

NOTE_____

_____

_____

_____

_____

_____

_____

_____

_____

_____

Coffee Toffee Crunch Protein Shake

A delightful combination of coffee and toffee flavors topped with a crunchy texture and packed with protein for a delicious and satisfying frozen treat.

INGREDIENTS

- 1 cup coffee protein shake
- 1/2 cup milk of choice
- 1/4 cup crushed almonds (optional, for mix-ins)
- 1 tablespoon toffee bits (optional, for mix-ins)

Prep Time: 5 minutes Skill Level: Easy

Freezing Time: 24 hours Servings: 1

INSTRUCTIONS

1. Blend: Combine protein shake and milk in a blender. Blend until smooth.
2. Freeze: Pour the mixture into a Ninja Creami pint, ensuring not to overfill. Freeze for at least 24 hours, or until completely solid.
3. Process: Place the frozen pint in your Ninja Creami Deluxe and select the "Frozen Drink" function.
4. Mix-In (Optional): Create a small hole in the center of the frozen drink about 1 1/2 inches deep using a spoon. Add the crushed almonds and/or toffee bits and use the "Mix-in" program to incorporate them evenly.
5. Enjoy Sip on your indulgent Coffee Toffee Crunch Protein Shake.

HEALTH BENEFITS

- Provides a good source of protein for muscle growth and repair.
- Coffee provides antioxidants and a natural energy boost.
- Almonds offer healthy fats and additional protein.

HEALTHY TIPS

- Use a low-sugar or unsweetened coffee protein shake.
- You can make your own healthier toffee bits by chopping updates and almonds.

Nutritional Information (Per Serving): Calories: 280 | Fat: 12g | Carbs: 25g | Protein: 22g

NOTE_____

_____

_____

_____

_____

_____

_____

Gingerbread Protein Shake

This is not your grandma's gingerbread – this protein-packed frozen treat captures the warm, spicy flavors of the holiday season with a cool, creamy twist. Perfect for a festive indulgence that won't derail your fitness goals.

INGREDIENTS

- 1 cup gingerbread protein shake
- 1/2 cup milk of choice
- 1/4 teaspoon ground ginger (optional, for extra spice)
- 1/4 cup crushed gingersnaps (optional, for mix-ins)

Prep Time: 5 minutes Skill Level: Easy

Freezing Time: 24 hours Servings: 1

INSTRUCTIONS

1. Blend: Combine gingerbread protein shake, milk, and additional ginger (if using) in a blender. Blend until smooth and creamy.
2. Freeze: Pour the mixture into a Ninja Creami pint, ensuring not to overfill. Freeze for at least 24 hours, or until completely solid.
3. Process: Place the frozen pint in your Ninja Creami Deluxe and select the "Frozen Drink" function.
4. Re-Spin (Optional): Re-spin once or twice for a creamier consistency.
5. Mix-In (Optional): Create a small hole in the center of the frozen drink about 1 1/2 inches deep using a spoon. Add crumbled gingersnaps and use the "Mix-in" program to incorporate them evenly.

HEALTH BENEFITS

- It is a very good source of protein for muscle growth and for repair.
- Ginger and spices offer potential anti-inflammatory benefits.
- May help to curb sweet cravings in a healthier way.

HEALTHY TIPS

- Choose a gingerbread protein shake with minimal added sugar.
- For a vegan version, use a plant-based protein shake and milk alternative.
- If you are sensitive to spice, you can omit the additional ground ginger.

Nutritional Information (Per Serving):
Calories: 200 | Fat: 5g | Carbs: 25g | Protein: 18g

Strawberry Shortcake Protein Shake

A creamy, protein-packed twist on the classic strawberry shortcake dessert. Enjoy the sweet and refreshing flavors of strawberries and cream with a boost of protein for a satisfying treat.

INGREDIENTS

- 1 cup vanilla protein shake
- 1/2 cup milk of choice
- 1 cup frozen strawberries
- 1/4 cup crumbled graham crackers (for mix-ins)

Prep Time: 5 minutes Skill Level: Easy

Freezing Time: 24 hours Servings: 1

INSTRUCTIONS

1. Blend: Combine protein shake, milk, and frozen strawberries in a blender. Blend until smooth and creamy.
2. Freeze: Pour the mixture into a Ninja Creami pint, ensuring not to overfill. Freeze for at least 24 hours, or until completely solid.
3. Process: Place the frozen pint in your Ninja Creami Deluxe and select the "Frozen Drink" function.
4. Re-Spin (Optional): Re-spin once or twice for a creamier consistency.

5. Mix-In (Optional): Create a small hole in the center of the frozen drink about 1 1/2 inches deep using a spoon. Add the crumbled graham crackers and use the "Mix-in" program to incorporate them evenly.

HEALTH BENEFITS

- Strawberries provide vitamin C and antioxidants, which are important for immune system support and skin health.
- Protein shake promotes muscle recovery and satiety, keeping you feeling full and energized.

HEALTHY TIPS

- Use a low-sugar or unsweetened vanilla protein shake for a healthier option.
- If you prefer a thicker shake, use frozen milk instead of regular milk.
- Add a scoop of Greek yogurt for make it more creamy and extra protein.

Nutritional Information (Per Serving): Calories: 200 | Fat: 5g | Carbs: 25g | Protein: 20g

Black Forest Protein Shake

A decadent frozen treat inspired by the classic Black Forest cake, this protein shake blends rich chocolate with tart cherries for a luxurious and nutritious indulgence.

INGREDIENTS

- 1 cup chocolate protein shake
- 1/2 cup milk of choice
- 1/2 cup frozen dark sweet cherries
- 1/4 cup frozen raspberries or strawberries
- 1/4 teaspoon almond extract
- 1/4 cup dark chocolate shavings (for mix-ins)

Prep Time: 5 minutes Skill Level: Easy

Freezing Time: 24 hours Servings: 1

INSTRUCTIONS

1. Blend: Combine chocolate protein shake, milk, frozen cherries, frozen berries, and almond extract in a blender. Blend until smooth and creamy.
2. Freeze: Pour the mixture into a Ninja Creami pint, ensuring not to overfill. Freeze for at least 24 hours, or until completely solid.
3. Process: Place the frozen pint in your Ninja Creami Deluxe and select the "Frozen Drink" function.
4. Re-Spin (Optional): Re-spin once or twice for a creamier consistency.
5. Mix-In: Create a small hole in the center of the frozen drink about 1 1/2 inches deep using a spoon. Add the dark chocolate shavings and use the "Mix-in" program to incorporate them evenly.

HEALTH BENEFITS

- Cherries provide antioxidants and may help reduce inflammation.
- Protein shake promotes muscle recovery and satiety.
- Chocolate contains flavonoids, which may have heart-health benefits.

HEALTHY TIPS

- Use unsweetened or low-sugar chocolate protein shake.
- Choose frozen cherries without added sugar.

Nutritional Information (Per Serving):
Calories: 230 | Fat: 5g | Carbs: 30g | Protein: 20g

"Awaken your inner warrior with every protein-packed."

recipe

Pink Lemonade Protein Slushy

A tangy and refreshing slushy with a pink hue, packed with protein for a boost after a workout or on a hot day.

INGREDIENTS

- 1 cup frozen raspberries
- 1/2 cup lemonade (low-sugar or homemade)
- 1 scoop unflavored or vanilla protein powder
- 1 tablespoon chia seeds (optional, for mix-ins)
- Squeeze of lemon juice (optional)

Prep Time: 5 minutes Skill Level: Easy

Freezing Time: 24 hours Servings: 1

INSTRUCTIONS

1. Blend: Combine all ingredients (except chia seeds) in your Ninja Creami blender until smooth.
2. Freeze: Pour the mixture into a Ninja Creami pint and freeze for at least 24 hours.
3. Process: Place the frozen pint into the Ninja Creami Deluxe and select the "Slushy" function.
4. Re-Spin (Optional): Re-spin once or twice for a smoother consistency.
5. Mix-In (Optional): Create a small hole in the center of the slushy about 1 1/2 inches deep using a spoon. Add chia seeds and use the "Mix-in" program to incorporate them evenly.
6. Re-spin (Optional): Re-spin once or twice for a smoother consistency.

HEALTH BENEFITS

- Raspberries are packed with antioxidants and fiber.
- Protein powder supports muscle recovery and satiety.
- Hydrating and refreshing.

HEALTHY TIPS

- Use unsweetened lemonade or make your own for a healthier option.
- If you like your slushy tart, add an extra squeeze of lemon juice.
- Chia seeds add fiber and omega-3 fatty acids.

Nutritional Information (Per Serving):
Calories: 150 | Fat: 1g | Carbs: 25g | Protein: 12g

Pineapple Mango Protein Slushy

A tropical explosion of flavor, this sweet and tangy slushy is a perfect way to cool down and get a boost of protein.

INGREDIENTS

- 1 cup frozen pineapple chunks
- 1 cup frozen mango chunks
- 1/2 cup water or coconut water
- 1/2 scoop vanilla protein powder
- 1/4 cup shredded coconut (unsweetened, optional for mix-ins)

Prep Time: 5 minutes Skill Level: Easy

Freezing Time: 24 hours Servings: 2

INSTRUCTIONS

1. Blend: Combine all ingredients (except for the optional shredded coconut) in the Ninja Creami blender until smooth.
2. Freeze: Pour the mixture into a Ninja Creami pint, ensuring not to overfill. Freeze for at least 24 hours, or until completely solid.
3. Process: Place the frozen pint in your Ninja Creami Deluxe and select the "Slushy" function.
4. Mix-In (Optional): Create a small hole in the center of the slushy about 1 1/2 inches deep using a spoon. Add shredded coconut and use the "Mix-in" program to incorporate them evenly.
5. Re-Spin (Optional): Re-spin once or twice for a smoother consistency.

HEALTH BENEFITS

- Mango and pineapple are rich in vitamins, minerals, and antioxidants.
- Protein powder supports muscle recovery and satiety.
- Coconut adds healthy fats and electrolytes.

HEALTHY TIPS

- Make sure you use fresh or frozen fruit for the best flavor.
- Choose a protein powder with minimal added sugar.

Nutritional Information (Per Serving):
Calories: 200 | Fat: 5g | Carbs: 30g | Protein: 15g

NOTE_____

_____

_____

_____

_____

_____

_____

_____

Sweet Cream Protein Slushy

A creamy and luscious slushy reminiscent of a classic vanilla milkshake, elevated with protein for a guilt-free indulgence.

INGREDIENTS

- 1 cup milk of choice
- 1 scoop vanilla protein powder
- 1/4 cup heavy cream
- 2 tablespoons sweetener of choice (e.g., honey, maple syrup)
- 1/4 teaspoon vanilla extract
- Crushed cookies or sprinkles (optional, for mix-in)

Prep Time: 5 minutes Skill Level: Easy

Freezing Time: 24 hours Servings: 1

INSTRUCTIONS

1. Blend: Combine milk, protein powder, heavy cream, sweetener, and vanilla extract in the Ninja Creami blender. Blend until smooth and creamy.
2. Freeze: Pour the mixture into a Ninja Creami pint, ensuring not to overfill. Freeze for at least 24 hours, or until completely solid.
3. Process: Place the frozen pint in your Ninja Creami Deluxe and select the "Slushy" function.
4. Mix-In (Optional): Create a small hole in the center of the slushy about 1 1/2 inches deep using a spoon. Add crushed cookies or sprinkles. Use the "Mix-in" program to incorporate them evenly.
5. Re-Spin (Optional): Re-spin once or twice for a smoother consistency.

HEALTH BENEFITS

- Provides a good source of protein for muscle growth and repair.
- Calcium from the milk supports bone health.

HEALTHY TIPS

- Use unsweetened almond milk or low-fat milk for a lower-calorie option.
- Choose a high-quality protein powder with minimal added sugar.

Nutritional Information (Per Serving): Calories: 250 | Fat: 12g | Carbs: 20g | Protein: 20g

NOTE_____

_____

_____

_____

_____

_____

_____

Pineapple Green Tea Protein Slushy

A refreshing and unique blend of tropical pineapple and earthy green tea, infused with protein for a healthy and delicious slushy.

INGREDIENTS

- 1 cup frozen pineapple chunks
- 1/2 cup brewed green tea, chilled
- 1/2 scoop vanilla protein powder
- 1/4 cup water or coconut water
- Sweetener to taste (optional)

Prep Time: 5 minutes Skill Level: Easy

Freezing Time: 24 hours Servings: 1

INSTRUCTIONS

1. Blend: Combine all ingredients (except for optional mint leaves) in the Ninja Creami blender and blend until smooth.
2. Freeze: Pour the mixture into a Ninja Creami pint, ensuring not to overfill. Freeze for at least 24 hours, or until completely solid.
3. Process: Place the frozen pint in your Ninja Creami Deluxe and select the "Slushy" function.
4. Re-Spin (Optional): Re-spin once or twice for a smoother consistency.

HEALTH BENEFITS

- Pineapple is a very good source of Vitamin C with bromelain, an enzyme with anti-inflammatory properties.
- Green tea provides antioxidants and L-thiamine, an amino acid that promotes relaxation.
- Protein powder supports muscle recovery and satiety.

HEALTHY TIPS

- Use unsweetened or freshly brewed green tea for a lower sugar content.
- If you prefer a sweeter slushy, add a natural sweetener like honey or agave.

Nutritional Information (Per Serving): Calories: 180 | Fat: 3g | Carbs: 22g | Protein: 14g

NOTE

_____
_____
_____
_____
_____
_____
_____
_____
_____
_____
_____

Peachy Protein Zing

A revitalizing and refreshing slushy bursting with the sweetness of peaches, a hint of ginger spice, and a protein punch for sustained energy.

INGREDIENTS

- 1 cup frozen peach slices
- 1/2 cup unsweetened almond milk
- 1/2 scoop vanilla protein powder
- 1/4 teaspoon ground ginger
- 1/4 cup chopped crystallized ginger (optional, for mix-ins)

Prep Time: 5 minutes Skill Level: Easy

Freezing Time: 24 hours Servings: 1

INSTRUCTIONS

1. Blend: Combine all ingredients (except for the optional crystallized ginger) in the Ninja Creami blender until smooth.
2. Freeze: Pour the mixture into a Ninja Creami pint, ensuring not to overfill. Freeze for at least 24 hours, or until completely solid.
3. Process: Place the frozen pint in your Ninja Creami Deluxe and select the "Slushy" function.
4. Re-Spin (Optional): Re-spin once or twice for a smoother consistency.
5. Mix-In (Optional): Create a small hole in the center of the slushy about 1 1/2 inches deep using a spoon. Add chopped crystallized ginger and use the "Mix-in" program to incorporate them evenly.

HEALTH BENEFITS

- Peaches are a good source of vitamins A and C.
- Ginger aids in digestion and has anti-inflammatory properties.
- Protein powder provides a boost of energy and helps with muscle recovery.

HEALTHY TIPS

- Use unsweetened almond milk for a lower-calorie option.
- Adjust the amount of ginger to your preference for spice level.

Nutritional Information (Per Serving): Calories: 180 | Fat: 4g | Carbs: 25g | Protein: 15g

NOTE_____

_____

_____

_____

_____

_____

_____

_____

_____

_____

Green Machine Protein Slush

A vibrant and nutritious, slushy that packs a punch of greens, tropical fruit, and protein for a healthy and refreshing treat.

INGREDIENTS

- 1 cup spinach or kale
- 1/2 cup frozen pineapple chunks
- 1/2 banana
- 1 scoop vanilla protein powder
- 1/2 cup coconut water
- 1/4 cup chopped walnuts or pecans (optional, for mix-ins)

Prep Time: 5 minutes Skill Level: Easy

Freezing Time: 24 hours Servings: 1

INSTRUCTIONS

1. Blend: Combine all ingredients (except for optional mix-ins) in the Ninja Creami blender and blend until smooth and creamy.
2. Freeze: Pour the mixture into a Ninja Creami pint, ensuring not to overfill. Freeze for at least 24 hours, or until completely solid.
3. Process: Place the frozen pint in your Ninja Creami Deluxe and select the "Slushy" function.
4. Re-Spin (Optional): Re-spin once or twice for a smoother consistency.
5. Mix-In (Optional): Create a small hole in the center of the slushy about 1 1/2 inches deep using a spoon. Add chopped nuts and use the "Mix-in" program to incorporate them evenly.

HEALTH BENEFITS

- Packed with vitamins, minerals, and antioxidants from leafy greens and fruit.
- High in fiber, promoting digestive health.
- Protein powder supports muscle recovery and satiety.

HEALTHY TIPS

- Use a ripe banana for natural sweetness and a creamy texture.
- A squeeze of fresh lemon or limejuice adds a bright touch and helps preserve the green color.
- Do not be afraid to experiment with other leafy greens like romaine lettuce or collard greens.

Nutritional Information (Per Serving): Calories: 230 | Fat: 8g | Carbs: 30g | Protein: 20g

Raspberry Rosé Sparkler

A sophisticated and refreshing slushy that marries the sweetness of raspberries with the subtle floral notes of rosé wine and a boost of protein.

INGREDIENTS

- 1 cup frozen raspberries
- 1/2 cup rosé wine
- 1/4 cup lime juice
- 1/2 scoop unflavored protein powder
- Fresh raspberries or edible rose petals (optional, for mix-ins)

Prep Time: 5 minutes Skill Level: Easy

Freezing Time: 24 hours Servings: 1

INSTRUCTIONS

- Blend: Combine all ingredients (except for optional mix-ins) in the Ninja Creami blender until smooth.
- Freeze: Pour the mixture into a Ninja Creami pint, ensuring not to overfill. Freeze for at least 24 hours, or until completely solid.
- Process: Place the frozen pint in your Ninja Creami Deluxe and select the "Slushy" function.
- Re-Spin (Optional): Re-spin once or twice for a smoother consistency.
- Mix-In (Optional): Create a small hole in the center of the slushy about 1 1/2 inches deep using a spoon. Add fresh raspberries or edible rose petals and use the "Mix-in" program to incorporate them evenly.

HEALTH BENEFITS

- Raspberries are a good source of antioxidants, vitamin C, and fiber.
- Rosé wine contains antioxidants.
- Protein powder supports muscle recovery and satiety.

HEALTHY TIPS

- Choose a dry rosé wine for a lower sugar content.
- Use a high-quality unflavored protein powder without artificial sweeteners.

Nutritional Information (Per Serving): Calories: 160 | Fat: 1g | Carbs: 15g | Protein: 12g

NOTE_____

_____

_____

_____

_____

_____

_____

_____

Bellini Bliss Slushy

A light and bubbly slushy inspired by the classic Italian Bellini cocktail, this protein-packed version is a delightful way to enjoy the flavors of peaches and prosecco.

INGREDIENTS

- 1 cup frozen peach slices
- 1/2 cup prosecco
- 1/4 cup peach nectar
- 1/2 scoop unflavored protein powder
- Fresh peach slices (optional, for mix-ins)

Prep Time: 5 minutes Skill Level: Easy

Freezing Time: 24 hours Servings: 1

INSTRUCTIONS

1. Blend: Combine all ingredients (except for the optional peach slices) in the Ninja Creami blender until smooth.
2. Freeze: Pour the mixture into a Ninja Creami pint, ensuring not to overfill. Freeze for at least 24 hours, or until completely solid.
3. Process: Place the frozen pint in your Ninja Creami Deluxe and select the "Slushy" function.
4. Re-Spin (Optional): Re-spin once or twice for a smoother consistency.
5. Mix-In (Optional): Create a small hole in the center of the slushy about 1 1/2 inches deep using a spoon. Add peach slices and use the "Mix-in" program to incorporate them evenly.

HEALTH BENEFITS

- Peaches provide vitamins, minerals, and antioxidants.
- Protein powder supports muscle recovery and satiety.

HEALTHY TIPS

- Choose a dry prosecco for a lower sugar content.
- Use unsweetened peach nectar or fresh peaches for a healthier option.

Nutritional Information (Per Serving):
Calories: 170 | Fat: 0g | Carbs: 20g | Protein: 10g

NOTE_____

_____

_____

_____

_____

_____

_____

_____

_____

_____

Dragon Fruit Lime Zing Slush

A vibrant and tangy slushy with a tropical twist, featuring the exotic flavor of dragon fruit, zesty lime, and a protein boost.

INGREDIENTS

- 1 cup frozen dragon fruit chunks
- 1/2 cup limeade (low-sugar or homemade)
- 1/2 scoop unflavored protein powder
- Lime zest or slices (optional, for mix-ins)

Prep Time: 5 minutes Skill Level: Easy

Freezing Time: 24 hours Servings: 1

INSTRUCTIONS

1. Blend: Combine all ingredients (except for the optional lime zest or slices) in the Ninja Creami blender until smooth.
2. Freeze: Pour the mixture into a Ninja Creami pint, ensuring not to overfill. Freeze for at least 24 hours, or until completely solid.
3. Process: Place the frozen pint in your Ninja Creami Deluxe and select the "Slushy" function.
4. Re-Spin (Optional): Re-spin once or twice for a smoother consistency.
5. Mix-In (Optional): Create a small hole in the center of the slushy about 1 1/2 inches deep using a spoon. Add lime zest or lime slices and use the "Mix-in" program to incorporate them evenly.

HEALTH BENEFITS

- Dragon fruit is packed with antioxidants and fiber.
- Limejuice provides vitamin C and supports immune function.
- Protein powder supports muscle recovery and satiety.

HEALTHY TIPS

- Use a low-sugar or sugar-free limeade for a healthier option.
- Choose a high-quality unflavored protein powder without artificial sweeteners.
- Add a few frozen raspberries for a beautiful color swirl and extra antioxidants.

Nutritional Information (Per Serving): Calories: 140 | Fat: 1g | Carbs: 22g | Protein: 12g

"Create culinary masterpieces that fuel your ninja lifestyle."

Discard the dairy and embrace a world of plant-powered protein! Your Ninja Creami is not just for whey anymore. Discover how to create luscious, creamy frozen treats that are not only delicious but also packed with the muscle-building, hunger-satisfying goodness of plant-based protein.

The Vegan Protein Pantry

Forget bland and boring, vegan protein sources are bursting with flavor and diversity. Pea, hemp, rice, soy, and other plant-based protein powders are your secret weapons for creating Ninja Creami masterpieces.

Creamy Vegan Secrets

Achieving a luxurious, scoopable texture with plant-based ingredients is easier than you think! Here are a few tips to make your vegan Ninja Creami protein delights dreams come true:

Soak and blend: Soak cashews, almonds, or other nuts before blending for extra creaminess.

Frozen bananas are your friend: Use frozen bananas as a base for instant creaminess and natural sweetness.

Embrace healthy fats: Add avocado, coconut cream, or nut butters for richness and flavor.

Do not skimp on the flavor: Use spices, extracts, and fresh or frozen fruit to create bold, delicious flavor profiles.

With these tips and tricks, you will be churning out vegan protein-packed Ninja Creami creations that rival any dairy-based dessert.

Keto Creami Craze

Who says you cannot have your Ninja Creami and eat it too? Even if you are watching your carbs or following a keto diet, you can still satisfy your sweet cravings with guilt-free frozen delights.

Sugar-Free Symphony

Bid farewell to blood sugar spikes! Swap traditional sugar with keto-friendly sweeteners like erythritol, stevia, or monk fruit. These natural alternatives provide sweetness without the carbs, allowing you to enjoy your favorite flavors without compromising your dietary goals.

Dairy-Free Delights

Discard the lactose and embrace the creaminess of low-carb milk alternatives like almond milk, coconut milk, or cashew milk. These dairy-free options not only reduce your carb intake but also add a unique flavor twist to your Ninja Creami creations.

Chocolate Avocado Fudge Pops

A guilt-free chocolate indulgence. These fudgy pops are surprisingly creamy and rich, thanks to the healthy fats in avocado. They are also packed with antioxidants and fiber.

INGREDIENTS

- 1 ripe avocado, pit and skin removed, chopped
- 1/4 cup unsweetened cocoa powder
- 1/4 cup erythritol (or your preferred keto sweetener)
- 1 cup unsweetened almond milk (or other low-carb milk)
- Mix-in Options: Chopped nuts, sugar-free chocolate chips

Prep time: 10 minutes Skill level: Easy

Freezing time: 24 hours Servings: 4

INSTRUCTIONS

1. Blend all the base ingredients: In the Ninja Creami blender, combine avocado, cocoa powder, erythritol, and almond milk. Blend until completely smooth.
2. Pour and freeze: Pour the mixture into a Ninja Creami pint container and freeze for at least 24 hours.
3. Process: Process the frozen mixture by pressing the "Ice Cream" function of the Ninja Creami Deluxe machine.
4. Re-spin (optional): For an even creamier texture, press the "Re-spin" function.
5. Mix-ins (optional): Create a hole about 1 1/2 inches deep with a spoon in the ice cream and pour your desired mix-in. Use the "Mix-in" program to distribute it evenly.

HEALTHY TIP

- For extra richness, add a tablespoon of nut butter to the base ingredients.

HEALTH BENEFITS

- Avocado is a very good source of healthy fats, fiber, and vitamins.
- Cocoa powder is rich in antioxidants.
- Erythritol is a sugar alcohol that does not raise blood sugar levels.

Nutrition Information (per serving): Calories: 150 Protein: 3g Fat: 12g Net Carbs: 5g

NOTE_____

_____

_____

_____

_____

_____

Strawberry Cheesecake Ice Cream

A creamy, dreamy keto dessert. This low-carb ice cream tastes like a slice of strawberry cheesecake, but without the guilt.

INGREDIENTS

- 4 ounces cream cheese, softened
- 1 cup frozen strawberries
- 1/4 cup erythritol (or your preferred keto sweetener)
- 1/2 teaspoon vanilla extract
- Mix-in Options: Chopped nuts, sugar-free granola

Prep time: 5 minutes Skill level: Easy

Freezing time: 24 hours Servings: 2

INSTRUCTIONS

1. Blend all the base ingredients: In the Ninja Creami pitcher, combine cream cheese, frozen strawberries, erythritol, and vanilla extract. Blend until smooth.
2. Pour and freeze: Pour the mixture into a Ninja Creami pint container and freeze for at least 24 hours.
3. Process: Process the frozen mixture by pressing the "Ice Cream" function of the Ninja Creami Deluxe machine.
4. Re-spin (optional): For an even creamier texture, press the "Re-spin" function.
5. Mix-ins (optional): After processing, create a hole in the ice cream and add your desired mix-ins.

HEALTHY TIP

- For a richer flavor, use full-fat cream cheese.

HEALTH BENEFITS

- Strawberries are a good source of antioxidants and vitamin C.
- Cream cheese provides protein and calcium. Erythritol does not raise blood sugar levels.

Nutrition Information (per serving): Calories: 200 Protein: 5g Fat: 16g Carbs: 6g

Vanilla Bean Ice Cream

A classic flavor with a keto twist. This simple recipe highlights the pure flavor of vanilla beans without the added sugar.

INGREDIENTS

- 2 cups unsweetened almond milk (or other low-carb milk)
- 1 vanilla bean, split and scraped
- 1/4 cup erythritol (or your preferred keto sweetener)

- Mix-in Options: Chopped nuts, sugar-free chocolate chips.

Prep time: 5 minutes Skill level: Easy

Freezing time: 24 hours Servings: 2

INSTRUCTIONS

1. Blend all the base ingredients: In the Ninja Creami pitcher, combine almond milk, scraped vanilla bean seeds, and erythritol. Blend until smooth.
2. Pour and freeze: Pour the mixture into a Ninja Creami pint container and freeze for at least 24 hours.
3. Process: Process the frozen mixture by pressing the "Ice Cream" function of the Ninja Creami Deluxe machine.
4. Re-spin (optional): For an even creamier texture, press the "Re-spin" function.
5. Mix-ins (optional): After processing, create a hole in the ice cream and add your desired mix-ins.

HEALTHY TIP

- For a richer flavor, use full-fat coconut milk.

HEALTH BENEFITS

- Vanilla beans have anti-inflammatory properties.

- Almond milk is a very good source of vitamin E.

Nutrition Information (per serving): Calories: 120 Protein: 2g Fat: 9g Net Carbs: 5g

Lemon Coconut Cream Pops

A Sunshine-Kissed Keto Refreshment: Escape to a tropical paradise with these tangy, creamy pops—the perfect blend of bright citrus and rich coconut, without the carb overload.

INGREDIENTS

- 1/2 cup full-fat coconut cream
- 1/4 cup of fresh squeezed lemon juice (from 1 large lemon)
- 1 tablespoon of lemon zest (from 1 large lemon)
- 1/4 cup powdered erythritol (or your preferred keto sweetener, adjust to taste)
- Mix-in Options (After Processing): Finely chopped fresh berries, shredded unsweetened coconut.

Prep Time: 5 minutes

Freezing Time: 24 hours

Skill Level: Easy

INSTRUCTIONS

1. Blend the Base: Combine the coconut cream, lemon juice, lemon zest, and

erythritol. Blend until completely smooth and well combined.

2. Freeze the Base: Pour the mixture into a Ninja Creami pint container, ensuring it is evenly distributed. Securely fasten the lid and freeze for at least 24 hours, or until completely solid.

3. Process into Pops: Once frozen, remove the pint container from the freezer and take off the lid. Place the container into the outer bowl of the Ninja Creami Deluxe. Select the "ice cream" setting and press start.

4. Re-Spin for Extra Creaminess: For an even smoother, creamier texture, run the "Re-spin" function after the initial processing cycle is complete.

5. Incorporate Mix-ins (Optional): If desired, carefully create a hole about 1 1/2 inches deep with a spoon in the center of the processed mixture. Gently spoon your chosen mix-ins into the hole. Use the "Mix-in" program to distribute them evenly throughout the pops.

HEALTHY TIPS

- Fresh is Best: Use freshly squeezed lemon juice and zest for the most vibrant flavor and aroma.

- Adjust Sweetness: Taste the mixture before freezing and adjust the erythritol to your liking.

HEALTH BENEFITS

- Coconut Cream: Provides healthy fats that support satiety and energy levels.

- Lemon Juice & Zest: Bursting with vitamin C, an antioxidant that boosts immunity and skin health.

Nutrition Information (per serving): Calories: 80 Protein: 0g Fat: 8g Carbs: 3g

Ninja Creami Hacks

Elevate your keto-friendly Ninja Creami game with these clever hacks:

- Thicken with chia seeds: Add a tablespoon of chia seeds to your mixture for extra creaminess and a boost of fiber.

- Experiment with flavors: Incorporate sugar-free chocolate chips, keto-friendly caramel sauce, or a sprinkle of cinnamon for added depth of flavor.

- Top with keto-friendly treats: Chopped nuts, berries, or a drizzle of sugar-free chocolate syrup make delicious and nutritious topping

ACKNOWLEDGEMENT

From my kitchen to yours, this cookbook would not be here without the incredible support I have received. You, dear readers, your enthusiasm for healthy, nutritious Ninja Creami creations has been my constant motivation. Your willingness to embrace this new way of creating frozen treats fills my heart with joy.

To my amazing family and friends who turned into taste testers, your honest opinions and endless encouragement have been invaluable. You have helped me refine and perfect these recipes, ensuring they are both mouthwatering and good for you.

A huge shout out to the Ninja team! You have truly revolutionized the way we create frozen treats with the Ninja Creami Deluxe. Your innovative machine has made it so easy for everyone to whip up incredible frozen treats that are actually healthy. I am honored to be able to share recipes that take full advantage of this amazing invention.

In addition, of course, my deepest gratitude goes to the talented individuals. Your guidance, expertise, and unwavering belief in this project have brought it to life. Your dedication to quality shines through on every page.

Your feedback is a gift, so please, do not hesitate to leave an honest review and let me know what you loved most about the book!

With heartfelt thanks,

ANN J. BRYNER

	Breakfast	*Lunch*	*Dinner*
Sunday	Peachy Protein Dream Ice Cream	Fruity Fiesta Protein Shake	Tropical Protein Punch Sorbet
Monday	Tropical Protein Paradise Sorbet	Pineapple Coconut Protein Swirl Ice Cream	Minty Chocolate Chip Protein Shake
Tuesday	Watermelon Mint Refresher Ice Cream	Coffee Lover's Protein Pick-Me-Up	Tart Cherry Protein Power Sorbet
Wednesday	Raspberry-Lime Protein Fizz Sorbet	Oatmeal Cookie Protein Shake	Peanut Butter Cup Obsession Ice Cream
Thursday	Minty Chocolate Chip Protein Ice Cream	Citrus Sunshine Protein Lite Ice	Double Chocolate Malt
Friday	Salted Caramel Mocha Protein Lite Ice	Cookies & Cream Protein Dream Ice Cream	Cookies & Cream Protein Overload
Saturday	Chocolate Brownie Batter Protein Shake Ice Cream	Lunch: Almond Joy Protein Shake	Matcha Coconut Cream Protein Lite Ice

	Breakfast	Lunch	Dinner
Sunday	Strawberry Cheesecake Protein Shake Ice Cream	Raspberry Cheesecake Protein Shake	Tropical Piña Colada Protein Lite Ice
Monday	Low Carb Mint Madness Protein Lite Ice	Mango Pineapple Protein Shake	Berry Balsamic Protein Swirl Gelato
Tuesday	Strawberry Kiwi Protein Swirl Gelato	Pink Lemonade Protein Slushy	Low-Calorie Brownie Chunk Protein Lite Ice
Wednesday	Citrus Buzz Protein Creamiccino	Greek Yogurt Protein Base	Tropical Passion Fruit Gelato
Thursday	Vegan Vanilla Protein Base	Stracciatella Protein Gelato	Protein Coffee Lite Ice Cream
Friday	Vanilla Chai Protein Shake Gelato	Tropical Protein Yogurt Delight	Raspberry Cocoa Protein Creamiccino
Saturday	Peach Melba Swirl	Caramel Apple Protein Creamiccino	Honey Lavender Protein Gelato

NINJA CREAMI RECIPE TRACKER

Recipe Title

Date:

INGREDIENTS	QUANTITY	NOTE

Base Recipe

Ice cream [ ]   Other [ ]

Adjustment (extract, spices)

Ninja creami settings

Churn time_____

Re-spin yes/no, if yes how many times_____

Texture

Smooth & Creamy [ ]

Slightly Icy [ ]

Chunky [ ]

Prep Time_____Minutes

Freezing Time_____Hours

No of Serves

Nutritional Info (per serving)

Remarks

_____

_____

_____

_____

_____

_____

Recipe Title

Date:

INGREDIENTS	QUANTITY	NOTE

Base Recipe

Ice cream [ ]   Other [ ]

Adjustment (extract, spices)

Ninja creami settings

Churn time_____

Re-spin yes/no, if yes how many times_____

Texture

Smooth & Creamy [ ]

Slightly Icy [ ]

Chunky [ ]

Prep Time_____Minutes

Freezing Time_____Hours

No of Serves

Nutritional Info (per serving)

Remarks

_____
_____
_____
_____
_____
_____
_____
_____

Recipe Title

Date:

INGREDIENTS	QUANTITY	NOTE

Base Recipe

Ice cream [ ]   Other [ ]

Adjustment (extract, spices)

Ninja creami settings

Churn time_____

Re-spin yes/no, if yes how many times_____

Texture

Smooth & Creamy [ ]

Slightly Icy [ ]

Chunky [ ]

Prep Time_____Minutes

Freezing Time_____Hours

No of Serves

Nutritional Info (per serving)

Remarks

_____

_____

_____

_____

_____

_____

_____

_____

Recipe Title

Date:

INGREDIENTS	QUANTITY	NOTE

Base Recipe

Ice cream [ ]   Other [ ]

Adjustment (extract, spices)

Ninja creami settings

Churn time_____

Re-spin yes/no, if yes how many times_____

Texture

Smooth & Creamy [ ]

Slightly Icy [ ]

Chunky [ ]

Prep Time_____Minutes

Freezing Time_____Hours

No of Serves

Nutritional Info (per serving)

Remarks

_____

_____

_____

_____

_____

_____

_____

_____

Recipe Title

Date:

INGREDIENTS	QUANTITY	NOTE

Base Recipe

Ice cream [ ]   *Other [ ]*

Adjustment (extract, spices)

Ninja creami settings

Churn time_____

Re-spin yes/no, if yes how many times_____

Texture

Smooth & Creamy [ ]

Slightly Icy [ ]

Chunky [ ]

Prep Time_____Minutes

Freezing Time_____Hours

No of Serves

Nutritional Info (per serving)

Remarks

_____

_____

_____

_____

_____

_____

_____

_____

Recipe Title

Date:

INGREDIENTS	QUANTITY	NOTE

Base Recipe

Ice cream [ ]   Other [ ]

Adjustment (extract, spices)

Ninja creami settings

Churn time_____

Re-spin yes/no, if yes how many times_____

Texture

Smooth & Creamy [ ]

Slightly Icy [ ]

Chunky [ ]

Prep Time_____Minutes

Freezing Time_____Hours

No of Serves

Nutritional Info (per serving)

Remarks

_____

_____

_____

_____

_____

_____

_____

APPENDIX 1: RECIPE INDEX

Almond Joy Protein Shake 80

Banana Bread Protein Shake   95

Bellini Bliss Slushy   107

Berry Balsamic Protein Swirl   27

Berry Banana Protein Yogurt Delight   59

Berry Banana Protein Yogurt Delight   63

Berry Vanilla Protein Swirl Sorbet 39

Black Forest Protein Shake   99

Blueberry Muffin Protein 84

Build-Your-Own Protein Shake   83

Caramel Apple Protein Creamiccino   87

Chocolate Avocado Fudge Pops   110

Chocolate Banana Protein 74

Chocolate Brownie Batter Protein Shake Ice 23

Chocolate Peanut Butter Protein Sorbet   38

Chunky Monkey Protein Gelato   35

Citrus Buzz Protein   85

Citrus Sunshine protein Lite Ice   47

Coconut Cardamom Protein Bliss   73

Coconut Cream Protein Pie   71

Coffee Caramel Protein Ice Cream 26

Low-Calorie Brownie Chunk Protein Lite Ice   52

Cookies & Cream Protein Overload   79

Creamiccino   85

Creamy Coconut Sorbet   40

Coffee Lover's Protein Pick-Me-Up   76

Coffee Toffee Crunch Protein Shake   96

Cookies & Cream Protein Dream Ice Cream   22

Double Chocolate Malt   78

Dragon Fruit Lime Zing Slush   108

Dragon Fruit Protein Delight 65

Frozen Protein Mudslide   91

Fruity Fiesta Protein Shake   75

Gingerbread Protein Shake   97

Greek Yogurt Protein Base   55

Green Machine Protein Shake   94

Green Machine Protein Slush 105

Green Protein Fro-Yo   61

Hazelnut Chocolate Swirl Protein Gelato   34

High-Protein Parfait   58

Honey Lavender Protein Gelato   31

Horchata Protein Spice   70

Keto Coffee Gelato 33

Lemon Coconut Cream Pops 112

Low Carb Mint Madness Protein Lite Ice   51

Maple Cinnamon Latte Protein Creamiccino 89

Matcha Coconut Cream Protein Lite Ice 49

Minty Chocolate Chip Protein Ice Cream 21

Minty Chocolate Chip Protein Shake 75

Mixed Berry Protein Refresher 72

Oatmeal Cookie Protein Shake 77

Peach Melba Swirl 57

Peachy Protein Dream Ice Cream 17

Peachy Protein Zing 104

Peanut Butter Cup Obsession Ice Cream 20

Pineapple Coconut Protein Swirl Ice Cream 18

Pineapple Green Tea Protein Slushy 103

Pineapple Jalapeno Protein Surprise 67

Pineapple Mango Protein Slushy 101

Pink Lemonade Protein Slushy 100

Probiotic Protein Boost 60

Protein Blast Berry Mix Sorbet 43

Protein Coffee Lite Ice Cream 54

Protein Powerhouse Pistachio 32

Pumpkin Spice Protein Creamiccino 88

Raspberry Cheesecake Protein Shake 81

Raspberry Cocoa Protein Creamiccino 86

Raspberry Rosé Sparkler 106

Raspberry-Lime Protein Fizz Sorbet 46

Root Beer Protein Float 69

Salted Caramel Mocha Protein Lite Ice Protein 48

Spiced Apple Protein Cider 6

Spiced Pear & Ginger Protein Shake 93

Stracciatella Protein 29

Strawberry Cheesecake Ice Cream 111

Strawberry Cheesecake Protein Shake Ice Cream 24

Strawberry Kiwi Protein Swirl 28

Strawberry Lemonade Protein Fusion 66

Strawberry Shortcake Protein Shake 98

Strawberry Summer Sorbet 41

Sunrise Protein Smoothie 90

Sweet Cream Protein Slushy 102

Tart Cherry Protein Power Sorbet 44

Tropical Passion Fruit 29

Tropical Piña Colada Protein Lite Ice 50

Tropical Protein Paradise Sorbet 43

Tropical Protein Punch Sorbet 37

Tropical Protein Yogurt Delight 56

Vanilla Bean Ice Cream 111

Vanilla Bean Protein Ice Cream 25

Vanilla Chai Protein Shake 30

Vegan Vanilla Protein Base 53

Watermelon Mint Refresher Ice Cream 19

APPENDIX 2: CONVERSION CHART

VOLUME EQUIVALENT (DRY)

US Standard Measurement	Metric Equivalents
1/4 teaspoon	1.23 ml
1/2 teaspoon	2.46 ml
3/4 teaspoon	3.69 ml
1 teaspoon	4.93 ml
2 teaspoons	9.86 ml
1 tablespoon	14.79 ml
1/4 cup	59.15 ml
1/2 cup	118.3 ml
3/4 cup	177.45 ml
1 cup	236.6 ml
2 cups	473.2 ml
3 cups	709.8 ml
4 cups	946.4 ml

VOLUME EQUIVALENT (LIQUID)

US Standard (Imperial)	Metric (SI)
1 fluid ounce (fl oz)	29.574 milliliters (ml)
1 cup	236.588 milliliters (ml)
1 pint (16 fl oz)	473.176 milliliters (ml)
1 quart (32 fl oz)	946.353 milliliters (ml)
1 gallon (128 fl oz)	3.785 liters (L)
1 tablespoon	14.787 milliliters (ml)
1 teaspoon	4.929 milliliters (ml)
1 milliliter (ml)	0.0338 fluid ounces (fl oz)
1 liter (L)	33.814 fluid ounces (fl oz)
1 liter (L)	1.0567 quarts
1 liter (L)	0.26417 gallons

TEMPERATURE EQUIVALENT

Fahrenheit (°F)	Celsius (°C)
225 °F	107 °C
250 °F	120 °C
275 °F	135 °C
300 °F	150 °C
325 °F	160 °C
350 °F	180 °C
375 °F	190 °C
400 °F	205 °C
425 °F	220 °C
450 °F	235 °C
475 °F	245 °C
500 °F	260 °C

WEIGHT MEASUREMENT

Ingredient	US Standard	Metric
1/2 ounce	14.175 grams	
1 ounce	28.35 grams	30 mL
2 ounces	60 grams	60 mL
5 ounces	150 grams	150 mL
10 ounces	300 grams	300 mL
16 ounces	450 grams	450 mL
1 pound	454 grams	454 mL
1.5 pounds	681 grams	681 mL
2 pounds	907 grams	907 mL

Made in the USA
Coppell, TX
29 November 2024

41281788R00070